Salman Rushdie's Early Fiction

# Salman Rushdie's Early Fiction

UMA PARAMESWARAN

RAWAT PUBLICATIONS
Jaipur • New Delhi • Bangalore • Mumbai • Hyderabad • Guwahati

ISBN 81-316-0072-6




*Published by*
Prem Rawat for **Rawat Publications**
Satyam Apts., Sector 3, Jawahar Nagar, Jaipur 302 004 (India)
Phone: 0141 265 1748 / 7006 Fax: 0141 265 1748
E-mail: info@rawatbooks.com
Website: www.rawatbooks.com

*New Delhi Office*
4858/24, Ansari Road, Daryaganj, New Delhi 110 002
Phone: 011-23263290

*Also at Bangalore, Mumbai, Hyderabad and Guwahati*

Typeset by Rawat Computers, Jaipur
Printed at Chaman Enterprises, New Delhi

For
my Mother, who lived and loved the era
of
*Midnight's Children*
and
my Father, whose way of reading *Midnight's Children* gave me an understanding of the method and meaning of the perforated sheet. He would open the book at random and read on until he was interrupted or fell asleep.

# Contents

# Preface

My earlier book on Rushdie's fiction, *The Perforated Sheet: Essays on Salman Rushdie's Art* (Chennai: East-West Books) dealt with Rushdie's first three works of fiction – *Grimus, Midnight's Children* and *Shame*. Its publication in the Autumn of 1988 almost exactly coincided with the release of *The Satanic Verses*. Because of the furor that followed *The Satanic Verses*, it is understandable that the publisher did not promote my book with much zeal. It is now out of circulation. Between 1988 and 1994, I presented papers at various conferences and published several more essays.

This volume brings together many of the papers I published or presented between 1982 and 1998, including much of the contents of the earlier volume. I have reproduced the essays as they were published, except for a few minor revisions. Therefore, there is some repetition of data. Since 1998, I have left Rushdie behind as it were, and gone on to focus on my own fiction-writing. Much has been published on Rushdie in the last decade, but I trust this volume will be of some use as an introduction to his fiction.

I am appreciative of Mr. Pranit Rawat of Rawat Publications for publishing this volume.

University of Winnipeg **Uma Parameswaran**

# Acknowledgements

The following essays were published in a slightly different version in the following journals and volumes:

1. Biographical Highlights [A slightly different version of this was written for the 2004 Edition of *Encyclopedia of Postcolonial Literatures in English.* Eds. Benson and Connolly (Routledge)]
2. Autobiography as History: Saleem Sinai and India in Rushdie's Midnight's Children [*Toronto South Asian Review* 1:2 (Summer, 1982)]
3. Handcuffed to History: Salman Rushdie's Art [*Ariel 14:4* (October 1983)]
4. "Lest he Returning chide": Saleem Sinai's Inaction in Salman Rushdie's *Midnight's Children* [*The Literary Criterion* XVIII:3 (1983)]
5. Salman Rushdie in Indo-English Literature [*The Journal of Indian Writing in English* 12:2 (July 1984)]
6. The Perforated Sheet: Method as Meaning in *Midnight's Children* (1988) [Chapter 5 of my earlier work, *The Perforated Sheet: Essays on Salman Rushdie's Art*]

7. New Dimensions Courtesy of the Whirling Demons: Word-Play in *Grimus* [*Reading Rushdie: Perspectives on the fiction of Salman Rushdie.* Edited By D.M. Fletcher. Amsterdam: Rodopi. 1993.]
8. An Analysis of *Shame* [Chapter VII of *The Perforated Sheet,* 1988.]
9. Salman Rushdie's *Shame*: An Overview of a Labyrinth (1990) [*The New Indian Novel in English: A Study of the 1980s*. Ed. Viney Kirpal. Bombay: Allied Publishers. 1990.]
10. Impressive Women but the Chains are no Fictions: Women in Rushdie's *Shame* [*Women in Indo-Anglian Fiction: Tradition and Modernity.* Ed. Naresh K. Jain. New Delhi: Manohar. 1998. pp. 141-157.]
11. Girl Children in Rushdie's Fiction [Chapter 28 in *The Girl Child in 20th Century Indian Literature*. Ed. Viney Kirpal. New Delhi: Sterling Publishers. 1992.]
12. Purdah in Salman Rushdie, Attia Hosain and Rama Mehta [*Margins of Erasure: Purdah in the Subcontinental Novel in English.* Ed. Jasbir Jain and Amina Amin. New Delhi: Sterling Publishers. 1995.].
13. The We/They Paradigm in Rushdie's *The Satanic Verses* [US/THEM: *Translation, Transcription and Identity in Post-Colonial Literary Cultures.* Ed: Gordon Collier. Amsterdam: Rodopi. 1992.]
14. A Review of a Text (*TSAR,* 1993)

# 1

# Biographical Highlights

## Rushdie, Salman (born 1947)

### *Indian Novelist*

Born on June 19, 1947 in Mumbai, India, to Negin and Anis Ahmed Rushdie, Salman was the eldest of four siblings. He and his three sisters grew up in Mumbai. In 1961, he was sent to Rugby School, England. From Rugby, Rushdie went to Cambridge University, where he took a degree in history in 1968. He lived in England from 1961 to 2000, except for brief visits to India and Pakistan. He has been married four times, to Clarissa Luard, Marianne Wiggins, Elizabeth West, and is now married to Padma Lakshmi. He has two sons, Zafar and Milan, born seventeen years apart. He now lives in the United States.

Rushdie is the author of eleven works of fiction – *Grimus* (1975), *Midnight's Children* (1981), *Shame* (1983), *The Satanic Verses* (1988), *Haroun and the Sea of Stories* (1990), *The Wizard of Oz* (1992),

---

A slightly different version of this was written for the 2004 Edition of *Encyclopedia of Postcolonial Literatures in English.* Eds. Benson and Connolly (Routledge)

*East West*(short stories, 1994), *The Moor's Last Sigh* (1995), The *Ground Beneath her Feet* (1999) and *Fury* (2001); *Shalimar the Clown* (2005); a documentary on Nicaragua titled *The Jaguar Smile: A Nicaraguan Journey* (1987), and numerous literary reviews and essays, the best of which have been collected in *Imaginary Homelands* (1991) and *Step Across this Line: Collected Non Fiction* (2002).

The Ayatolla Khomeini passed the death sentence (fatwah) on Rushdie on 14 February 1989 on the grounds that *The Satanic Verses* represents a blasphemy against the Koran. On Sept. 25, 1998, the Iranian government lifted the fatwah. Rushdie moved to the United States early in 2000.

All of Rushdie's novels are characterized by an epic sweep of narration, a plethora of allusions to real events, real people, mythological and literary characters, and hilarious, often ribald humour reminiscent of Rabelais and Tristram Shandy. Rushdie combines realism and fantasy, and, like South American novelists Gabriel Garcia Marquez and Jorge Luis Borges, he roundly satirizes the politics and society of the country in which each novel is set. He has also been compared to Gunter Grass. Among his Indian-English literary kin, one thinks of G. V. Desani and Raja Rao, both of whom experiment with Indianizing English through syntax, translated idiom, and word coinage, and who adapt the Hindu epic form of narration which, like a Russian doll set, reveals an almost endless cluster of stories within stories.

Several themes recur in Rushdie's writing. He himself identifies the theme of emigration and the migrant self as his favourite leitmotif. In *Shame*, and especially in *The Satanic Verses*, he expatiates on the baggage that immigrants bring with them and that weighs them down. His novels are an indictment on political evils: on prejudice within the British immigration department, which abuses and abases non-white residents; on the 1980s race riots in Brixton, England, which he calls Brickhall; and on police brutality. The central issues in all his novels are the dichotomy of good and evil in oneself and the world, philosophical speculation about faith, and the role of will power in visionary experience.

In what may be called the India-trilogy (*Midnight's Children, Shame* and *The Satanic Verses*) Rushdie uses a standard pattern – he explores the philosophical significance of ideals and concepts through several pairs of characters who are so intimately connected that they literally or figuratively fuse, and when they separate each takes on a part of the identity of the other. Thus, in Rushdie's first novel, *Grimus,* Flapping Eagle the Amerindian protagonist and Grimus the satanic antagonist literally fuse and then break away. The twin characters in *Midnight's Children,* Saleem Sinai and Shiva, are born in adjoining hospital rooms on the stroke of midnight at the moment of India's independence on 14-15 August 1947. The twin characters in *Shame,* Hyder Raza and Iskander Harappa, are fictional re-creations of President Zia-ul-Haq and Prime Minister Zulfikar Ali Bhutto. Rushdie's characterization of Harappa's daughter is a prophetic though unflattering sketch of Benazir Bhutto's charisma and rise to power. *Shame,* predictably, was banned in Pakistan. In most of Rushdie's novels, good overcomes the evil force, or at least survives. Even in the novels that end in cataclysmic annihilation (*Grimus* and *Shame*) or apparent hopelessness (*Midnight's Children*), this element of good surviving over evil is so strong that one might well call Rushdie a romantic who uses the medium of satire in his early novels.

Rushdie's satire is virulent, especially in *The Satanic Verses.* Here he satirizes Islamic fundamentalism – hence the uproar in the Muslim world that resulted in the Ayatollah's fatwah. There are three distinct stories, not successfully intertwined. The main one is that of two actors, Gibreel Farishta of Bombay, who has acted in numerous scriptural movies of all faiths, and Saladin Chamcha of London, who is a stage radio actor. The second story is that of Mahound, a fictionalized rendition of Prophet Muhammad, the founder of Islam. This part consists of two chapters totalling about seventy pages of the 547 pages in the novel. The third story is that of a beautiful mystic called Ayesha, who leads her villagers to the Arabian Sea where, she has been told by the Archangel Gabriel, the waters will part so they can walk over to Mecca, the holy city. The waters do not part and everyone is drowned.

The title, *The Satanic Verses,* refers to two apocryphal verses in the Koran: one about the Prophet being instructed to allow worship of the three major goddesses of the old dispensation –

Lat, Uzza, and Manat – alongside Allah, and the second about him being instructed soon afterwards that the first had been the voice of Satan and that God would not admit worship of any heathen goddesses.

The narrative strategy that Rushdie uses is to represent the entire story as sequences from the dreams and nightmares of Gibreel Farishta as he broods over possible movie productions. However, this narrative ploy did not gain him reprieve from the ire of fundamentalist Muslim readings. Examples of misreading and misconstrued translations that have fanned the flames of fundamentalism abound. Since one of the traditional synonyms for the Koran is 'verses', the adjective 'satanic' in the title has been seen as qualifying the Koran rather than just the two apocryphal verses. Similarly, though the novel speaks of the whores of Jahilia *imitating* the appearance and idiosyncrasies of the Prophet's wives, it is generally read by fundamentalist Muslims as slandering the real wives of the real Prophet.

The controversy over *The Satanic Verses* has shown that the cross-cultural chasms, that have always posed problems in the reading of new literatures in English, have assumed enormous proportions in such areas as comparative western and Islamic ideas of social responsibility and freedom of speech in literature.

Though his stylistic exuberance and magical realism continue undiminished, the novels written after the fatwah lack the energy and vision of the India trilogy. The protagonists are world weary, moving towards darkness. The violence that is seen through a panoramic lens in the earlier novels is seen up close, and gets more graphic with each novel. *The Moor's Last* Sigh repeats the theme of good versus evil, and the commentary on India's politics, through Moraes Zogoiby, who is stricken with a disease that ages his body at twice the normal rate. As in *Midnight's Children,* the narrator is under sentence of death, but since this novel was written while Rushdie was in hiding, one sees personal and political parallels. As in *Shame,* the setting is a decaying mansion with many rooms, and the characters act out matriarch Epifania's curse that a house divided against itself cannot stand. . At the national level, the allusions reach out to the communal riots that periodically rock India. Farther behind stands the fort of Alhambra in Granada, where Moraes' ancestor, Sultan Boabdil, sadly realized that Moors and the Spanish could never co-exist in harmony.

His next novel, *The Ground Beneath Her Feet,* is yet another extravaganza. It begins with the death of Vina Apsara on the fourteenth of February, 1989, the day of the Fatwah. As in *Shame* and *The Satanic Verses,* there are two concurrent plots that do not quite come together. One is the mythic overhang of Orpheus and Eurydice, relived through Ormuz Cama and Vina Apsara, both of whom have grisly childhoods. The other is an exuberant celebration of rock music and of America.

*Fury (2001)* is the first novel that is set wholly in the west. Professor Malik Solanka, who has left England for New York in search of a space where he could leave the past behind, is both world weary and given to uncontrollable rage and amnesia. Rushdie has said in an interview that fury is "not entirely destructive, [but] also a creative force." It is often born of "the discrepancy between promises and actualities . . . the gap between what we're led to believe is possible" and the lives we actually lead.

*Shalimar the Clown* (2005) returns to India. Though his innovative prose style and fast pace are as strong in this as in other novels, regrettably Rushdie's downward spiral continues in this work. Perhaps it is the repetition that palls, perhaps it is the author trying too hard to live up to his literary reputation in the face of diminishing inspiration. Characterization is rather shallow, and even the magic realism does not come through. The triangle that Indo-English writers seem to be obsessed with is front, back and centre – Shalimar is a Muslim; he is in love with Boonyi, a Hindu, and his rival is Jewish Max Ophuls, who instead of being the usual Brit as in *Midnight's Children,* is the American ambassador to India. The novel is like a James Bond movie script, full of action, violence, womanizing. There are the usual autobiographical elements, the usual references to world happenings. What is not usual is the characters' failure of moral responsibility, which leaves the author in a rather disturbingly vulnerable position of seeming to condone the main characters' terrorist acts and militant inclinations.

Since moving to the United States, Rushdie has published regularly in major newspapers on world happenings, on events in the Middle East and the aftermath of the terrorist bombing of the World Trade Centre on September 11, 2001.

# 2

# Autobiography as History

## Saleem Sinai and India in Rushdie's *Midnight's Children*

"Indo-English literature . . . is a bastard child of Britain and a British colony, having, characteristically enough, Christian missionaries as foster parents," I wrote in the opening paragraph of my study of representative Indo-English novelists that was published in 1976. This figurative statement is evidently true of the first Indo-English poet, Henry Derozio (1809-1831), whose father was Indian and mother English, and who was inspired by his Indian environment but in diction and style copied the minor romantics of England. His poetic descendants through the nineteenth century and early twentieth – Toru Dutt, Romesh Chunder Dutt, Manmohan Roy – wrote in the same vein; it is only with Rabindranath Tagore's poetry and fiction that we see the emergence of a predominantly Indian inspiration and language.

---

This essay was published in *Toronto South Asian Review* 1:2 (Summer, 1982) pp.52-60

Salman Rushdie's *Midnight's Children* expresses this metaphorical connection in a very literal way – Saleem Sinai, the writer-protagonist, is the son of an Englishman who has seduced the wife of a Hindu street singer. He is educated at the Cathedral and John Connon's Boys' High School in Bombay. He writes an autobiography that in its delineation of boyhood is as poignant as W.O. Mitchell's *Who has seen the Wind*, as authentic as Mark Twain's *Huckleberry Finn* and as ribald as Roth's *Portnoy's Complaint*. The novel is a landmark in Indo-English literature, and Saleem's parentage is symbolic of his connection to the literature he has enriched. It is interesting to note that the author's biography, in its bare outline, highlights another facet of identity that characterizes this novel – cross-cultural interactions and divided loyalties between Hindus and Muslims, India and Pakistan. Rushdie was born (in June 1947) in India, his parents emigrated to Pakistan after he left for England (in 1961), and he now lives in Britain.

The link between Saleem Sinai and Indo-English literature is a significant one. But it is only one aspect of the many-stranded chain of linked sequences in the novel. The strand that I would like to deal with here is that of Saleem and Indian history. *Midnight's Children* is mainly an autobiography of Saleem Sinai, but it is also the history of India during the period of the action. Rushdie links these in two ways: through events in Saleem's life that are actually connected to contemporary events through himself or one of his circle of friends or family; and through having significant events in Saleem's life coinciding with political events of historical importance.

Rushdie has thus hit upon an ingenious literary device. The linking is not always effective, but nevertheless the novel is eminently readable throughout.

The first event in the novel related to history is the Jallianwala Bagh massacre. In 1919, the government (this was during the British Raj, we must remember) passed the Rowlatt Acts, which gave it unlimited powers, including "doing away with ordinary legal procedure and authorizing imprisonment without trial" (R.C. Majumdar et.al., *An Advanced history of India* [Delhi: Macmillan, 1958], p. 984). Mahatma Gandhi called for nationwide protest meetings. On April 13, 1919, about 500,000 people assembled at Jallianwala Bagh, an enclosed park in Amritsar. General R.E. Dyer, Martial Law Commander of Amritsar, ordered his troops to fire. They "fired 1600 rounds of ammunition into the unarmed crowd that had no means of exit. Even according to official estimates 379 persons-were killed, and 1200 wounded" (ibid.). In *Midnight's Children,*

> Brigadier Dyer's fifty men put down their machine guns and go away. They have fired a total of one thousand six hundred and fifty rounds into the unarmed crowd.
>
> Of these, one thousand five hundred and sixteen have found their mark, killing or wounding some person.

Saleem's grandfather, Dr. Aadam Aziz, treats as many as he can.

This incident tells us two important things about Rushdie's handling of history: he is fairly accurate about the historical facts he uses; and he makes historical events of personal significance to Saleem by involving a member of his family in the event. One other point is that there may or may not be any apparent connection between the event and Saleem's life, but if one looks deeper one might find some significance; this incident, for instance, is related to Saleem's life at a later point.

The next historical event – or movement – is the rise and fall of Sheikh Abdullah, Sher-e-Kashmir (the Lion of Kashmir). While the Muslim League was firmly established and intent upon the creation of Pakistan, Sheikh Abdullah, a Kashmir Muslim, founded the Muslim National Conference, which leaned towards Gandhi's undivided India and against the Muslim League. Sheikh Abdullah lived long after Independence, but Rushdie's Mian Abdullah, founder of Free Islam Convocation, is killed by six assassins, "six crescent knives held by men dressed all in black," but before he dies there is a supernatural aura given to him. The Hummingbird, as he is called in the novel, hums his body into steel so that the "long curved blades had trouble killing him"; he hums in decibels beyond human hearing till all the glass in the windows shattered, till all the dogs in the city "came like wild things, leaping through the windows" and tore the assassins with their teeth so that "nobody could say who they were." The personal link in the story is Abdullah's secretary,

Nadir Khan, who escapes and seeks refuge at Aadam Aziz's house, and later marries Aadam's daughter Amina, who is forced to divorce him after two years when Aadam finds out that they have not yet consummated their marriage. (Amina then marries Ahmed Sinai, and Saleem is their son.)

August 14, 1947. Pakistan came into being a moment past the midnight of August 13. And Vanita, Wee Willie Winkie's wife, who had been seduced by Methwold, starts her labour pains at exactly the same moment. Twenty-four hours later, on the stroke of midnight as India entered freedom, she gives birth to a ten-pound baby boy. At the same moment, in the same nursing home, Amina Sinai gives birth to a baby – also male, also ten pounds. Mary Pereira, bamboozled by her lover's Marxist ideas, switches babies, contributing her bit to the leveling up of society's haves and have-nots. Thus Vanita (Mother India) and William Methwold (England) have brought into existence Saleem (Pakistan); this parallel does not hold all the way unless one is to see the Sinais as representative of Jawaharlal Nehru, the Kashmiri who unwittingly condemned India (Shiva) to a life of destitution and faulty ideology. Saleem grows up in the luxury of the Sinai household while the real Sinai baby, Shiva, grows up in the slums.

The assassination of Mahatma Gandhi is mentioned in passing, but nothing of historical significance is dwelt upon until the linguistic reorganization of states late in 1956. Dr. Narlikar, the doctor who delivered Saleem, has ambitions of reclaiming land from the sea by making stilts with a line of concrete tetrapods and then building upon it; this is a joint project by Ahmed and the doctor, and they place the first of the tetrapods on an embankment overlooking the sea. One day, while Narlikar is looking at his concrete brainchild, irate language marchers push him out of their way; he is pushed into the sea, still clinging to the concrete tetrapod, which soon drowns him. His drowning is Saleem's first experience of death. It is linked to the linguistic division of the country, perhaps one of the worst political decisions made. Narlikar's death is also linked more personally to the beginning of the financial and moral degeneration of Saleem's father. Of the national implications, Saleem says,

> India had been divided anew, into fourteen states and six centrally administered territories. But the boundaries of these states were not formed by rivers, or mountains, or any natural features of the terrain; they were, instead, walls of words. Language divided us.

Rushdie goes on to summarize the antagonism between Gujarati and Marathi-speaking people in the state of Bombay. One day, in a bicycle accident, Saleem is thrown in the midst of angry Marathi demonstrators; who taunt him to speak Gujarati. He repeats the only rhyme he knows – learnt from a Goanese schoolmate, Keith Colaco – which makes fun of the rhythms of Gujarati language patterns: "How are you? I am well. I'll take a stick and thrash you to hell." Thus Rushdie has Saleem as the originator of a popular slogan of the time. "In this way I became directly responsible for triggering off the violence which ended with the partition of the state of Bombay;" says Saleem. Though at the literary level the narrative is funny, its ironic intent is clear: major political events quite often have their sources in trivia.

In the spring of 1957, elections were held in India, and the Communist party won a large number of seats. Language oriented parties – such as the Marathi and Gujarati groups – divided the electorate, reducing still further the number of seats that the All India Congress had hoped to win.

There are two links more direct than the death of Suresh Narlikar between the story of Saleem and the story of India at this juncture. Shiva and Saleem's mother are partly responsible for the outcome of the election. Shiva and his gang, called "Cowboys," intimidate the voters, and later enter the polling booths, break open the ballot boxes and "fix" the results so that the Congress wins. Saleem identifies the Congress only indirectly: "only one party had really large sums to spend." The Communist cause is served by Saleem's mother, Amina Sinai. Amina has been meeting her ex-husband Nadir, whom she has never ceased to love. He has now become a Communist; she campaigns for him and his party, donating time and money to the destitute, who in return vote Communist.

Rushdie's links are a literary device and he uses it ingeniously. The elections of 1957 took place in the spring of the year but Saleem has his mother campaigning in the summer of 1957. The discrepancy is not an oversight, because Saleem realizes it, "And then it occurs to me that I have made another error – that the election of 1957 took place before, and not after; my tenth birthday." Thus Rushdie adds complexity to his narrative technique.

The next public event that occurs is the manslaughter of Homi Catrack, Lila Sabarmati's lover, by Commander Sabarmati of the Indian Navy. This incident was in the headlines of Indian magazines and newspapers at that time. The real names of Saleem's characters are well known to his contemporaries – as are the battles between the Navy and the Law as to whether Commander Nanavati should be in a civil jail or in naval custody. As with the language slogan, Saleem is personally responsible for triggering off the manslaughter, but whereas the former event was purely accidental, this one is premeditated, though Saleem obviously did not realize how serious his interference would become. Saleem, in order to teach his mother the lesson that she should stop her strange liaison with Nadir (they do not at any time have sexual intercourse), decides to expose another pair of lovers – Homi Catrack and Lila Sabarmati. Thus, a very personal problem precipitates a social and political scandal.

A similar personal link is present in the next story that Saleem has for us. His classmate, Cyrus Dubash, is made into a religious-cult leader by his widowed mother. He becomes Lord Khusro Khusrovand Bhagwan. The brief narrative of Lord Khusro's rise and fall is an amalgam of the stories of actual persons, such as Guru Maharaj, and Hatha Yogi Lakshman Rao who claimed he could walk on water. Other cult leaders, "Bhagwan" Rajneesh and Mahesh Yogi, also come to mind. Saleem claims to have been at the root of this cult and the evolution of Cyrus Dubash to whom he had loaned his Superman comic:

> the one containing the frame story, about the explosion of planet Krypton and the rocketship in which Jor-El his father despatched him through space, to land on earth and be adopted by the good, mild Kent.

Mrs. Dubash had read it and had set out to make her son a Superman of another mould. Saleem records

> [I] found myself obliged, yet again, to accept responsibility for the events of my turbulent, fabulous world.

With a similar tour de force, Rushdie links Jawaharlal Nehru's death to Saleem's grandfather. Dr. Aadam Aziz, angry at God for son Hanif's death, stalks off on Christmas Day, 1963 from his Agra home. On the 27th, "a man answering to my grandfather's description" was seen at a Srinagar mosque, from which the Prophet's hair disappeared next morning. Such an event actually did take place, and it sparked off communal riots within India and a diplomatic crisis between India and Pakistan. Rushdie, using all the tools of ambiguity, connects Saleem's grandfather to an event that took place in history. And then, stretching his tale still further, he connects the whole episode to Nehru's death with what might well be a tongue-in-cheek remark:

> After the death of grandfather, Prime Minister Jawaharlal Nehru fell ill and never recovered his health. This fatal sickness killed him on May 27, 1964.

But between 1958, when Commander Sabarmati stands trial, and 1964, when Nehru died, Saleem is in the forefront of political events in Pakistan, to which his mother had emigrated with her children – Saleem and the Brass Monkey, as he called his sister. They stay with Saleem's uncle, General Zulfikar, who plans General Ayub Khan's military takeover of the country. Saleem is at the midnight meeting of October 7, 1958 when Ayub Khan imposes Martial Law; three weeks later, Saleem is with his uncle when the General abducts President Iskander Mirza from his house and sends him to exile aboard a secret plane.

During the four years after the military takeover of Pakistan, Saleem does not participate in any historical event – either directly, or indirectly through a friend or relative. However, he records the important events in summary, as for example,

> Relations between India and Pakistan grew worse; entirely without my help, India conquered Goa ...[I] played no part

in the acquisition of large scale U.S. aid for Pakistan, nor was I to blame for Sino-Indian border skirmishes in the Aksai Chin region of Ladakh; the Indian census of 1961 revealed a literacy level of 23.7 per cent . . . and in the election of 1962, the All India Congress won 361 out of 494 seats in the Lok Sabha.

Amina Sinai and her children return to India in 1962 for a brief period while the Sino-Indian conflict is on, and for a very brief period it seems as though Saleem might still pull together the Midnight's Children's Conference that he had regularly convened in 1957-58; but it disintegrates.

The Sinais move permanently to Pakistan early in February 1963.

The war between India and China, with public reaction and newspaper headlines, is documented by Saleem, as also the infiltration of Pakistan into Kashmir and the subsequent Indo-Pakistani war of 1965. Saleem uses a series of ambiguous statements and questions to show how each side claimed all kinds of feats and conducted all kinds of treacheries. He uses factual accounts from newspapers and interweaves news of air raids with news of his own family, culminating in the night of September 22, 1965 when, in different places, all the members of his family die, except for Jamila Singer, his sister who is now a singing star, and Uncle Mustapha's family who are in Delhi.

Next, Saleem moves from 1965 to 1970, when he becomes a citizen of Pakistan. He is sent with sixty others to lead sixty thousand Pakistani soldiers in mufti to East Pakistan, which was about to secede and become Bangladesh. Saleem is their tracker, and like Bonzo the dog before him, he smells the terrain and leads the unit safely. Saleem's telepathic powers have been replaced by olfactory powers after an ear operation. Saleem records in passing that Indira Gandhi's New Congress Party had just won a landslide victory, with 350 out of a possible 515 seats in Lok Sabha.

On March 25, 1971, Saleem the tracker sniffs out Sheikh Mujibur Rahman, who is then arrested and flown to West Pakistan. Saleem also describes, in summary, the loot, rape and massacre of those days as the West Pakistani soldiers went on a rampage. Saleem, pretending to be chasing someone, runs away from the war area into the swamp area, the Sunderban. With him there are three others – all boy-soldiers; when they return to Dacca several weeks later, there are only two others, the third having been killed by a sniper's bullet.

Throughout the time that Saleem is in the invading army, he calls himself the Buddha and narrates in the third person. He is in a state of amnesia after his incestuous declaration to Jamila, but just how genuine the amnesia is remains an ambiguity. The name "Buddha" has two levels depending on its pronunciation, as he explains; his young colleagues call him "budda," with a hard d, meaning "old man," but he is also obviously the Buddha, the enlightened one. At this time, Saleem does not act. Shiva, on the other hand, acts quite unequivocally. Saleem's inaction, at the metaphoric level, connects to history, while it is also consistent with his personal problem. Saleem's inaction is related to Shiva's action; Shiva, of the Indian army, is described by a Bangladesh carpetbagger as:

> They have one mighty soldier fellow, he can kill six persons at one time, breaks necks *khrikk-khrikk* between his knees.

The episode has to be read thus: Shiva is actually the son of Ahmed and Amina Sinai; and Amina has always been a Pakistani at heart and she is at this time an immigrant in Pakistan. The Bangladesh episode in history was a civil war, the eastern arm of Pakistan rising against the west-based government and the western arm trying to put it down; it was a civil war – of Muslims killing fellow Muslims. Thus Shiva, born of Muslim parents and fighting for East Pakistan, is a Muslim killing his fellow Muslims. Saleem, who is actually of Hindu and English parentage, does not actively participate after betraying Sheikh Mujib. This betrayal might be linked, somewhat implausibly, to Saleem's English side, to Britain's divide-and-role policy that believed in causing trouble and ill will between two groups and then standing aside while they fought it out. Saleem's Indian side does not seem relevant to the episode in any historical context, since India went to great lengths to help Bangladesh refugees, even at the risk of depleting the national coffers. As Saleem records, India welcomed refugees and spent "$200,000,000 a month on refugees camps." Saleem, who has forgotten his name, is then found by Parvati-the-witch, another midnight child, in Dacca, where she has come as part of an entertainment crew for the

Indian soldiers. She calls him by name and thus recalls his identity to him. She arranges his escape, in a wicker basket, and they fly back to Delhi, arriving on February 23, 1973. On May 15, 1974, Major Shiva returns from the east and three days later meets Parvati. Major Shiva, a war hero, has had many liaisons, leaving a trail of bastard children among the rich and the poor; he now has a liaison with Parvati and abandons her once she gets pregnant. Shiva's increasing corruption can be paralleled to the deterioration of the country's economy and the corruption of its politicians under Indira Gandhi's government. The progress of Parvati's pregnancy is parallel to the growing strength of the Janata party under the leadership of Jaya Prakash Narayan and Morarji Desai. Parvati's labour pains start on June 12, 1975, the day the Allahabad High Court found Prime Minister Indira Gandhi guilty of two counts of campaign malpractice during the election of 1971:

> The thirteen days of Indira Gandhi's political career following this verdict see Parvati (who is, of course, Mother India) going through protracted labour pains, and the evening of the thirteenth day they screamed Yes, yes she has begun to push, come on Parvati, push push push, and while Parvati pushed in the ghetto, J.P. Narayan and Morarji Desai were also goading Indira Gandhi . . . so in a sense they were forcing Mrs. Gandhi to push . . . . (parenthetical insertion is author's)

And at midnight of June 25, 1975, just as Parvati brings forth her child, Indira Gandhi brings forth hers – Emergency Rule. The baby, Aadam, does not cry at all for the first year of his life, though he is tubercular; this parallels the nation's silent acceptance of the new dictatorship. Then, in 1976, Sanjay Gandhi, who had been a force behind the Prime Minister, stepped forward and rose to meteoric power. Two of his projects were carried out with swift and ruthless action: clearance of Delhi slums and pavements, and mass vasectomy camps to reduce population growth. Both are historical events, and Rushdie portrays both with racy and potent compression. He describes how vans and bulldozers break down the slum tenements and how quickly the slums transplanted themselves elsewhere. Anyone who was in

Delhi in the summer of 1976, as I was, would have witnessed the bulldozers clearing away the pavement shops of Karol Bagh, and similar sights elsewhere. Exactly as Rushdie says, the slums resurrected themselves as quickly as they were mown down. Rushdie ascribes magical powers to the magicians' ghetto, as it is called, but that is only one of his ways of recording history.

Sanjay Gandhi's second nationwide project was not so easily reversible – Vasectomy. Camps and units were set up everywhere and men vasectomized under force – bribed with radios or money, pressured into it by employers, or physically forced into it. Saleem describes the horrors in several passages, a surrealistic passage about the Widow's hand, a stoic excerpt on "what cannot be cured must be endured," and in pathetic, funny or horrifying reference to his own ectomization.

The last historical event mentioned in the novel is the election of 1977, when Indira Gandhi's Congress was defeated by the Janata Party. But Saleem does not foresee any permanence in a party, led by a wheel-chaired Jaya Prakash Narayan, and Morarji Desai. He has only the bleakest of prophecies for his son; and for future generations:

> Yes, they will trample me underfoot . . . reducing me to specks of voiceless dust, just as, all in good time, they will trample my son who is not my son, and his son who will not be his . . . until a thousand and one midnights have bestowed their terrible gifts and a thousand and one children have died because it is the privilege and the curse of midnight's children to be both masters and victims of their time . . . and to be unable to live or die in peace.

One should, perhaps, end this study with this, the last paragraph of the novel, for nothing is more powerful in modern storytelling than to end on a note of total hopelessness, an existential *nada,* but since this study attempts to correlate history and the narrative of a novel, one must end on a note of warning and observation – that Salman Rushdie's *Midnight's Children is* an excellent novel, that it gives us a variety of ideas and techniques, that it gives a fairly authentic history of contemporary India in the matter of facts, but that its interpretation of history is not always reliable.

# 3

# Handcuffed to History

## Salman Rushdie's Art

"THE EMPIRE WRITES BACK WITH A VENGEANCE," is the title of an article by Salman Rushdie in the London *Times of* July 3, 1982, in which he has written about the decolonizing of the English language by such writers as Chinua Achebe, Ngugi wa Thiong'o, Nadine Gordimer, Derek Walcott and R. K. Narayan. The title phrase embodies certain characteristics that dominate in Rushdie's writing: irony, showing here that erstwhile colonies of the British Empire should now be establishing supremacy in the development of English language and literature; word-play, building here the connotative network around both the title of the popular movie, "The Empire Strikes Back," and the Raj; and insight that zeroes in on the crux of an issue.

Salman Rushdie is clearly destined to be the subject of literary criticism for years to come. A study of his contribution to the decolonizing of English alone would fill a monograph. This essay, however, attempts to be no more than an introduction to his works, and to certain narrative techniques used in *Midnight's Children,* the novel that catapulted him to fame in 1981.

---

This essay was published in *Ariel 14:4* (October 1983), pp. 34-45.

Salman Rushdie was born in Bombay in June 1947[1]. He started his education at Cathedral School, Bombay. In 1961, he left for England, where he has lived ever since. He completed his schooling at Rugby, and later took a degree in history from King's College, Cambridge. He has worked with a multimedia theatre group, and an advertising company; he is now a full-time writer, working on freelance and commissioned articles for various newspapers and magazines. In 1964, Rushdie's parents, and presumably the rest of the family (he has three sisters), emigrated from India to Pakistan. Rushdie has made several trips to Pakistan, including an extended one of several months in 1975 (when he also visited India) just before starting on *Midnight's Children.* This novel took four and a half years to write, and was in the making for an even longer time.

Rushdie's other published works are a novel, *Grimus* (1975), and four short stories. His third novel, provisionally titled *Shame,* about half the length of *Midnight's Children* and set in Pakistan, is due for publication towards the end of 1983.

Two of his short stories are expanded versions of core ideas contained in *Midnight's Children;* there are dozens of potential short stories in the novel, and one might speculate that Rushdie might well develop or has already developed several of them; the episodes of the perforated sheet, the magicians' ghetto, Padma's misguided efforts at reviving Saleem's potency – these seem to be some of the author's favourites.

"The Prophet's Hair" is based on the same incident as the historical event included in the novel – a relic hair of the Prophet allegedly stolen from a Kashmir mosque, an event that set off communal clashes and caused a flare-up of Indo-Pakistani hostilities in 1964. Rushdie relates a fictionalized and far-fetched story with a combination of Arabian Nights fantasy (the illustrator's sketches adumbrate this) and raconteur humour. It is not without social satire, though. The power of the Prophet's hair cured the limbs of the sheikh's four sons, limbs that had been crushed conscientiously by the father in their infancy in order to assure them a good living – through begging. When cured, "they were, all four of them, very properly furious, because the miracle had reduced their earning power by seventy-five percent, at the worst conservative estimate; so they were ruined men."[2]

"The Free Radio"[3] is written in the style of R. K. Narayan, with an old *sadhu* type of school teacher as the narrative voice to comment on a gullible young rickshawallah who is doubly taken in by a widow with five children who did not want any more, and government propaganda that initially lured men into vasectomy by gifting a transistor radio to each volunteer. The young man habitually holds his imaginary radio to his ear, and hears "This is All India Radio," a fantasy that comes true for Saleem in a different way when he becomes a transmitting station, and is later forcibly vasectomized.

These two stories are readable but not particularly noteworthy. The first novel, *Grimus,* however, is a remarkable work. It seems fated to suffer a peculiar kind of oblivion, or step-brother recognition, because of the runaway success of *Midnight's Children. Grimus is* a rare combination of intellectual quibbling and gamesmanship with an earlier form of science fiction than is popular today.

Flapping Eagle (Born-from-dead), an Amerindian from Axona, drinks an elixir and wanders through seven centuries and innumerable sexual escapades (which are ever present in variegated patterns in Rushdie), and then falls through a hole in the Mediterranean and wakes up on Calf Island. Rushdie's conceptualization of another space-dimension is ingenious:

> Here we all are, a world of living beings and inanimate objects and gusts of breeze, all of us composed of infinitely more empty space than solid matter. Is it not a conceptual possibility that here, in our midst, permeating all of us and all that surrounds us, is a completely other world . . . with different perceptual tools which make us as non-existent to its inhabitants as they are to ours? In a word, another dimension.[4]

Similarly with Time, since there is always a Space-Time continuum in each world; the past, present and future coexist, and though ordinary human beings can move only in the present, there might be some (like the inhabitants of Calf Island) who can move from one dimension to the other.

The whole idea is consistent within its own terms, and is rather fascinating. However, it is too clever for its own good, as

Rushdie said of it.[5] The story line is a potpourri of Romance and lustful encounters. There is the Romantic archetype of the Wandering Jew. Like Ahaseurus, Flapping Eagle lives a long time (seven hundred and seventy-seven years plus) and sometimes longs for death, but unlike Ahaseurus, he is always young and virile. After 740 years of wandering he reaches Calf Island where he finds the Stone Rose, reminiscent of Arthurian romances and Tolkien, and undergoes a merging with the devil such as Dr. Faustus might have experienced if Rushdie were to rewrite Marlowe. But of course, everything in Rushdie is turned around to anti-Romance, anti-hero. Lustful encounters invariably end up as impotent ones and Cinderella as a pumpkin.

Word-play, another predominant Rushdie characteristic, runs rampant in *Grimus.* Grimus is an anagram of Simurg, the all-powerful mythic bird of Arab lore; the mountain of Calf is Kaf, an Arabic letter that has esoteric associations; Thera, Gorf, are self-evident anagrams, and Deggle's (part-clown, part-Mephistopheles) favourite word of leave taking is "Ethiopia" derived from "Abyssinia – I'll be seein' ya."

*Grimus* has several other characteristics in common with *Midnight's Children,* some of which are more fully developed and some vestigially present. Most important is the concept of a novel as propounded by Elfrida, one of the characters in *Grimus.* After listening to a story, she says:

> I don't like it . . . . It's too pretty, too neat. I do not care for stories that are so, so tight. Stories should be like life, slightly frayed at the edges, full of loose ends and lives juxtaposed by accident rather than some grand design. Most of life has no meaning – so it must surely be a distortion of life to tell tales in which every single element is meaningful? . . . How terrible to have to see a meaning or a great import in everything around one, everything one does, everything that happens to one! (*Grimus,* 149)

This statement epitomizes Rushdie's approach to the art of the novel when coupled with another, in *Midnight's Children*

> And there are so many stories to tell, too many, such an excess of intertwined lives events miracles places rumours, so dense a commingling of the improbable and mundane! I

> have been a swallower of lives; and to know me, just the one of me, you'll have to swallow the lot as well.[6]

The connection between the two statements is worth elaborating upon. The story to which Elfrida responds is about the Angel of Death, who finds that each soul he swallows becomes a part of him and he "begins to have doubts about whether he even exists as an independent being with all these people inside him" *(Grimus,* 149)

This amoeba-like fission and fusion is the distinguishing trait of the narrative voice or persona in both novels. In Grimus, we have Joe becoming a hermaphrodite through being christened Joe-Sue, and later becoming Flapping Eagle through an encounter with an eagle, and later merging into Grimus himself; throughout, though, there is an "I" that hasn't quite merged with the other aspect.

In *Midnight's Children,* there are two such characters. Tai the storyteller represents the synthesistic fusion of time-events; he is the repository of "racial memory," to use Yeats's term:

> I have watched the mountains being born; I have seen Emperors die . . . I saw that Isa, that Christ, when he came to Kashmir. Smile, smile, it is your history I am keeping in my head. *(MNC,*16)

Saleem represents this compression of history as a less harmonious process. Under alternating fission-fusion, his individual identity is by turn fragmented and enlarged by the "intertwined lives" around him; he becomes the repository of a national memory, if one might coin such a term.

The similarity between Rushdie and writers such as Garcia Marquez and Gunter Grass lies in this quality of mythic sweep that dislodges history from chronometric time in order to abstract its essential meaning, and disembodies individuals in order to extract the collective consciousness within.

Rushdie uses numerous narrative devices to connect Saleem's personal story with the story of India between 1947 and 1977. Three of the main structural devices are

(a) he uses birth images and metaphors to mark turning points in history and symbolize their long-term significance;

(b) he links political and historical events, starting with the Jallianwala Bagh massacre of 1919, with one or other of Saleem's circle of friends and family, and

(c) he uses Padma as a character who is functional at both narrative and symbolic levels.

Two other important techniques are Rushdie's use of irony and his periodic previews of events to come. The most pervasive element in his writing is, of course, his humour.

Birth images are Rushdie's obvious framework for linking autobiography with an interpretation of India's – recent history. "I had been mysteriously handcuffed to history, my destinies indissolubly chained to those of my country," says Saleem in the first page of *Midnight's Children,* referring to the coincidence of his birth with the birth of independent India on the stroke of midnight August 14-15, 1947. Saleem and the other one thousand infants born in that numinous hour of Independence are representative of the post-Independence generation born to promises of plenitude and fulfilment and later *chutneyfied* by circumstances and the Widow.

Shiva, his alter ego and rival, is the other person born on the stroke of midnight. Saleem's mother started her labour pains exactly twenty-four hours earlier, when Pakistan came into existence.

Saleem's wife's son, by Shiva, is born at midnight of the day when Indira Gandhi clamped down Emergency Rule on India. Parvati's thirteen-day labour coincides with the thirteen days of political tumult in India when Indira, found guilty of malpractice during the election of 1971, refused to resign and later proclaimed Emergency. Parvati and Saleem, Indira and India, each undergoes a traumatically long-drawn travail. The parallel between Parvati (and Saleem's) travail and India's is precise and nightmarish, ending with

> come on Parvati, push, push, push and while Parvati pushed in the ghetto, J. P. Narayan and Morarji Desai . . . . were forcing Mrs. Gandhi to push . . . . the Prime Minister was giving birth to a child of her own . . . . suspension of

> civil rights, and censorship of-the-press, and armoured-units-on-special-alert, and arrest-of subversive-elements. *(MNC, p. 419)*

Births and prognostications, births and symbols. Rushdie drives births home with a sledgehammer. Saleem is the son of an Englishman and a Hindu street-singer's wife; he is brought up by a Kashmiri Muslim couple whose own child is given to the street-singer by Mary, Pereira, a Goanese midwife who is influenced by her Marxist lover into doing her mite towards the equalization of classes; Mary Pereira, with her Catholicism and paranoia, becomes Saleem's ayah. The symbolism for religious friction, mixed ancestries, loss of identity, is very clear and very loud. So loud that one hesitates even to mention that we have in Saleem the writer, with his English father, Indian mother, Mission-schooling and Catholic ayah, an analogue of Indo-English writing.

Writing history as autobiography is another way of connecting the individual component of society with the collective stream of history. The fission-fusion element in the novel is most pervasive at this level.

*Midnight's Children,* at one level, is a Rabelaisian autobiography of Saleem Sinai whose Cyrano-nose, and adolescent sexuality get him into the usual scrapes of boyhood, and who later lives a Kafkaesque nightmare in a temporarily-totalitarian state. But Saleem's story has to be more than his own, linked indissolubly to his country's. The symbols used to link the autobiography of an individual to the history of a nation are obvious, sometimes heavy-handed.

Saleem's face is compared to the map of India by his school-teacher who, incidentally, also pulls out a handful of hair thus leaving a tonsure – Kashmir? – on his head. Saleem's telepathic contact with other Midnight Children, and their remarkable talents, reinforce the idea that the 1001 children are representative of India's post-independence generation, and that Saleem himself is their spokesman. Rushdie has said that the idea of placing Saleem centre-stage in so many political events came to him because a child usually sees himself centre-stage.[7]

(Obviously he has deeper reasons in the larger context of the novel.)

Rushdie's style is brilliant; he gallops through current newspapers, lancing headlines and sticking them on to the caps of relatives and friends so that the history of India reads like a family album. Saleem's uncle, Zulfkar, is a Pakistani general who helps General Ayub Khan plan the military takeover of 1958; his aunt is a mistress of Homi Catrack, who is shot by the husband of Lila Sabarmati, another of his mistresses (Commander and Mrs. Nanavati in real life); his classmate Cyrus Dubash becomes the founder of a religious cult that seems to be an amalgam of. Guru Maharaj and Hatha-yogi Lakshman Rao who claimed he could walk on water; Saleem himself triggers off one of the worst language riots in Bombay; his mother was first married to Sheikh Abdullah's right-hand man; the disappearance of the Prophet's Hair is linked to his grandfather the contrived connections go on.

There are several significant aspects of Rushdie's handling of history.[8] Through satire he shows that some of history's violent events have their source in trivial accidents as with the language demonstrations or the theft of the Prophet's Hair. At an overt level Rushdie spoofs the traditional form of histories. He takes liberties with dates, undermining chronometric exactitude that is one of the cornerstones of traditional historical writing. Saleem changes the date of Gandhi's death and of the 1957 election, but he does not retract when he realizes his error for "although I have racked my brains, my memory refuses, stubbornly, to alter the sequence of events" *(MNC,* 222). Memory reorders events.

> Rushdie also seems to spoof traditional histories for often being no more than biographies of kings and generals. The novel seems to say that the autobiography of a common man contains and participates in the making of history. Tai's claim that he was at Jehangir's deathbed is an extension of this participation.

However, what of the more specific connections between individual and nation? Saleem's thesis is clear: Ahmed Sinai's psychologically induced impotence becomes, by the Widow's decree, physical in Saleem; this physical impotence is the external manifestation of an inner impotence that has also, Salem implies, been imposed by the Widow.[9] But a closer reading of the novel would reveal that Rushdie has not quite succeeded in *showing* this strangulation as a long-drawn and consistent process. One is not convinced that the Midnight Children. themselves are not to blame for the betrayal of the dreams of 1947. Saleem Sinai's indictment of the "system" does not absolve him in our indictment of his inaction.

Saleem has argued his case in a way that would certainly sweep the unwary off their feet. With architectural balance and with insistent echoes and foreshadowings, he builds up his case against the government. Irony is his chief tool.

> Jawaharlal Nehru wrote: "Dear Baby Saleem, My belated congratulations on the happy accident of your birth . . . . we shall be watching over your life with the closest attention; it *will* be, in a sense, the mirror of our own . . . ." (*MNC*, 122)

The first Prime Minister's greeting ironically foreshadows the eagle-watch of a later prime minister which Saleem describes with frightening surrealism

> No colours except green and black the walls are green the sky is black (there is no roof) the stars are green the Widow is green but her hair is black as black. The Widow sits on a high high chair the chair is green the seat is black the Widow's hair has a centre parting it is green on the left and on the right black. High as the sky the chair is green the fingernails are long and sharp and black. Between the walls the children are green the walls are green the Widow's arm comes snaking down the snake is green the children scream . . . . the Widow's hand curls round them green and black. Now one by one the children mmff are stifled quiet the Widow's hand is lifting one by one the children green. . . the sky is black there are no stars the Widow laughs . . . . (*MNC*, 207)

But what did the children of this numinous hour, endowed with fantastic gifts of space-time travel and levitation, blinding beauty and genius, miracle-healing and computer-memory actually do? Nothing worthwhile. And little that even an untalented average person would care to boast about. For 28 years they frittered away their talent, and then with the rise of political repression in 1976, Saleem seems to have found a handy peg on which to hang all blame.

We are told in some detail what two of the most gifted Midnight Children did. Shiva, let it be said, never had any altruistic or patriotic concerns. He carried out his ideology: "Everybody does what I say or I squeeze the shit outa them with my knees" *(MNC,* 220). But Saleem had ideas, aspirations *and* unlimited opportunities; he had telepathic powers with which he could know others' thoughts and could communicate with those born in the same hour. He had strange olfactory powers. With his telepathic powers he toured India, went on voyeuristic binges, improved his grades by cheating, spied on his mother and aunt, gave no direction or leadership to the Conference, and finally betrayed the other Midnight Children to their murderers. With his olfactory powers, he whored all over Karachi and later betrayed Sheikh Mujibur Rahman of Bangladesh to his Pakistani enemies. It is this treason against himself, his teammates and basic ethics, that precludes any final sympathy for Saleem. There is no tragedy or sadness, only betrayal.

It has been said of modern novelists like Saul Bellow that their protagonists conclude on a note of qualified optimism that seems contrived because of the general bleakness of the final situation. With Saleem it is the other way around. Even though many aspects of his life seem to have taken a turn for the better after a decade of turmoil and suffering, he feels he has to end on a note of gloom:

> Yes, they will trample me underfoot . . . reducing me to specks of voiceless dust, just as, all in good time, they will trample my son who is not my son, and his son who will not be his . . . because it is the privilege and the curse of Midnight's Children to be both masters and victims of their times . . . to be unable to live or die in peace. *(MNC,* 463)

This extreme pessimism is uncalled for. Saleem's personal life has reached a level of stability: his son Aadam has outgrown his tuberculosis, has thrived on Durga's milk, and weaned himself off it with a suddenness that reflects his willpower for even at the age of twenty-two months he has a mind of his own.

The positive elements are all there, provided by the presence and services of Aadam, Picturesingh, Durga and the irreplaceable Padma.

Both Durga and Padma are earthy creatures, loud of mouth, generous in their giving. Durga, wet nurse and washerwoman, has preternatural breasts that could unleash "a torrent of milk capable of nourishing regiments." One might read into the choice of name to say she is both nourisher and destroyer, but her characterization is not such as to give her the attributes of the goddess. As a washerwoman, she "thrashed the life out of shirts and saris" and grew in power "as if she were sucking the vigour of the clothes, which ended up flat, buttonless and beaten to death." So also with her men.

On the other hand over Padma one could go into lyrical extremes, as Saleem does. But suffice it to say that she is a strong character in herself, and an excellent narrative prop and symbol. D. R. Sharma, writing in *New Quest,* is of another opinion

> How is the dumb interlocutor competent to absorb and examine a Niagara of subtle, erudite, metaphysical-cum-surrealistic interpolations of the narrative-historian? Even if Padma is removed from the book, the sweep or direction of the narrative won't be qualitatively impaired.[10]

Padma is not meant to absorb or examine. Literally and figuratively she is the haven that an artist needs in order to be an artist. Her role in the novel is very complex. She provides the climate, as said above; she provides the more immediate atmosphere as well, with her interjections, her comments on the narrative, her misguided efforts to get Saleem's "other pencil" to work, all of which add up to giving that realistic and tangible foil so necessary to keep the narrative to the ground.

It has been variously suggested that Padma is to be seen as *a vidushika* who in a Sanskrit play is a buffoon or jester who accompanies the hero; or as Rangeli in the Rangela-Rangeli team in folk theatre. I would suggest that if a dramatic analogue is to be taken, Padma is like the chorus in a Greek drama always on the stage, but never initiating action; essentially a non-participant but occasionally giving a thrust to the play's progression. But if the novel is dramatized, Padma would become quite a-problem for the director; with her well-endowed figure and "mammary-thumping" stance, she night become a stock-in-trade character of a typical Hindi movie, comical and exaggerated out of proportion. She would become wholly physical and literal, whereas in the novel she is both real and symbolic. She is – the collective consciousness, the spirit of the country, just as Saleem is an individual consciousness participating in the history of the country. Illiterate-but goodhearted, foolish yet wise, a devoted nurse but ever eager for the pleasure of the senses, Padma is the archetypal Earth-Mother put through the Rushdie anti-romance wringer.

Padma is Saleem's contact with the earth; she is the common people who, with their basic respect for learning (even though they might poke fun at "writery"), sustain the artist; the "real" human beings who will endure long after the Methwolds (Myth world), the affluent Sinais (desert-mountain-covenant of promised land – restrictive commandments) and brutish Shivas (Rushdie's understanding of Hindu names and archetypes leaves much to be desired) turn to dust.

## Notes

1. The biographical details included here were gathered from a talk by Salman Rushdie at Goteborg, Sweden, in September 1982.
2. Salman Rushdie, "The Prophet's Hair," *The Atlantic Monthly* (September 1981), 66.
3. Salman Rushdie, "The Free Radio," *The Atlantic Monthly* (June 1982), 75-77.
4. Salman Rushdie, Grimus (London: Granada, 1981), p. 55 *Grimus* was first published in 1975 by Victor Gollancz-Ltd.
5. "Interview: Salman Rushdie," *Kunapipi, IV,* 2 (1982), 25.
6. Salman Rushdie, *Midnight's Children,* 1982. London: Picador (Pan Books), p. g. (First published in 1981.) All subsequent quotations are from this edition and page references are given in parentheses.
7. See 1 above.

8. For a more detailed analysis of this theme, please refer to my article, 'Autobiography as History: Saleem Sinai and India in. Rushdie's *Midnight's Children*" *Toronto South Asian Review,* 1: 2 (Summer 1982), 52-60.
9. Rushdie's interpolation as to the identification of the Widow with Mrs.Indira Gandhi (p. 421) is in poor taste and is also an artistic weakness. Such explicit parallels are better left out of a novel, and left to critics!
10. D.R. Sharma, "Chutnification of India," *New Quest* (May-June 1982), 169.

# 4

# "Lest He Returning Chide"

## Saleem Sinai's Inaction in Salman Rushdie's *Midnight's Children*

Salman Rushdie's *Midnight's Children* (1981) is a remarkable work of fiction that is simultaneously a Rabelaisian autobiography of an individual and a Kafkaesque interpretation of India's contemporary history. It is safe to predict that the 1981 Booker Prize is only the first of many international distinctions in store for this novel[1].

Rushdie has carefully drawn numerous parallels between Saleem Sinai and his country, right from his face which resembles "the whole map of India"[2] to his fortune which is "indissolubly chained to those of my country" (9). Some of the links are too farfetched to be anything but spoofing on the author's part; some are so hilariously funny that they cannot be read as serious no matter bow one stretches them; but there are enough serious links to say that Rushdie has a serious purpose running through his novel. Two central references are the extra-ordinary talents of Midnight's Children and the nightmare

---

This essay was published in *The Literary Criterion* XVIII: 3 (1983) pp. 57-66.

of the Widow's hand.[3] The Widow's hand, Saleem implies, crushed the children. The symbolism is very clear in this surrealistic passage:

> "No colours except green and black the walls are green the sky is black (there is no roof) the stars are green the Widow is green but her hair is black as black. The Widow sits on a high high chair the chair is green the seat is black the Widow's hair has a centre parting it is green on the left and on the right black. High as the sky the chair is green the fingernails are long and sharp and black. Between the walls the children are green the walls are green the Widow's arm comes snaking down the snake is green the children scream – the Widow's hand curls round them green and black. Now one by one the children mmff are stifled quiet the Widow's hand is lifting one by one the children green . . . the sky is black there are no stars the Widow laughs (207)."

The irony in another key passage reinforces the same message: that the miraculous powers of those born in the hour of India's Independence are to be stifled by the powers that be:

> Jawaharlal Nehru wrote: 'Dear Baby Saleem, My belated congratulations on the happy accident of your moment of birth . . . . We shall be watching over your life with the closest attention; it will be, in a sense, a mirror of our own:'
>
> And Mary Pereira, awestruck "The Government Madam? It will be keeping one eye on the boy? But why, Madam? What's wrong with him?"

Mary's misinterpretation of the Prime Minister's greetings ironically foreshadows the iron fist of a later Prime Minister.

Quite apart from the invalidity or validity of this assessment as related to actual recent history, we must analyze if Salman Rushdie has succeeded in showing this strangulation within the literary framework of this novel. My contention is that Saleem Sinai, and his compeers, bury their talent in the ground instead of using it. They might ask, "Does God exact day labour light denied?" but light was denied them, if at all when they were twenty eight years old but by then they had already let their abilities dissipate or atrophy.

This paper traces how the Widow's hand, despite Saleem's claim, is not the cause of the failure of Midnight's Children within the novel but only the catalyst of another phase in their betrayal of themselves.

One thousand and one children were born between midnight and 1 a.m. on the night of August 14-15, 1947, that is, during the first hour of India's freedom from British rule.

> Owing to some preternatural power of the moment as though history, arriving at a point of the highest significance and promise, had chosen to sow, in that instant, the seeds of a future which would genuinely differ from anything the world had seen up to that time, the one thousand and one children born in that numinous hour were endowed with features, talents or faculties that can only be described as miraculous (195).

They were born in various parts of the country, and each had a different kind of talent: a boy in Kerala who could step into mirrors and reemerge from any reflective surface he wished; a girl in Goa who could multiply fish; twin sisters in Orissa who made men fall hopelessly in love with them on sight; a boy in Kashmir who could change his sex at will; a sharp-tongued girl near Calcutta who could inflict physical wounds just by a verbal abuse; a witch girl in Gir Forest who could heal by the laying-on of hands; a time traveler; one with computer-memory .... Those born near midnight had the most wonderful gifts of all. Parvati-the-witch, born seven seconds after midnight, was the daughter of the greatest conjurer in Oudh and has "genuine gifts of conjuration and sorcery"; Shiva who was born on the stroke of midnight presumably has the attributes of his divine namesake, "the god of destruction, whom no force could resist." Saleem, also born on the stroke of midnight got "the greatest talent of all – the ability to look into the hearts and minds of men" (200). Later he developed the sharpest olfactory powers, and could smell out persons, their clothes, their secretions, the different foods they had eaten that day.

Fantastic gifts, though the absence of poets, artists, scientists or even politicians is disturbing. Let us trace to what use these were put, especially by Saleem. As a baby, Saleem could read others' thoughts, such as: Ishaq coveting his brother's wife Nussie; Nussie's husband Ismail worrying over his legal career; Lila Sabarmati planning her infidelities. But only one person, Toxy Catrack the half-wit, ever 'nudged' his mind. Just what thoughts she sent into his baby head, he never did know, but the memory of her masturbation was to trigger off something during his first experience of his great gift.

The first time Saleem becomes conscious of his gifts is at the age of "nearlynine" in June 1956. Saleem has made the washing-chest (laundry basket with wooden slats) in his mother's bathroom his hideaway from the pressure of the expectations which others have of him. "Although the creature was inside me, the comforting presence of enveloping soiled linen seemed to lull it to sleep" (152). Though he is not aware of it, his mother had already started her strange liaison with her former husband, Nadir Khan, whom she had loved but had to divorce because they had not consummated their marriage even after two years. After one of the long telephone calls from him, she comes into the bathroom where Saleem is in his hideaway washing chest and she moans for her lover, "Arre Nadir Khan" and then, "summoned by a more trivial necessity" she seats herself on the commode – at which time Saleem sniffs in an effort to hold back a sneeze. His sinuses are "subjected to unbearable pressure until something bursts" in his head. He hears a deafening many-tongued voice inside his cranium.

> Sent into silent confinement for a day, Saleem continues to hear voices.
>
> By sunrise, I had discovered that the voices could be controlled-I was a radio receiver . . . , I could select individual voices; I could even, by an effort of will, switch off my newly-discovered inner ear (164).

Saleem tries to tell his parents about this phenomenon but they think it blasphemous that he should claim to hear voices – only the prophet could – and his father slaps him so hard his left ear gets impaired.

Saleem learns not to speak about his powers. He also learns to go beyond languages into the universally intelligible thought forms which far transcended words, and to understand what is spoken in the different languages of India by his receiving apparatus. His initial dismay and confusion are powerfully delineated; he reads the thoughts of those around him: his father mentally undressing his secretary, his uncle brooding over his failures, his ayah Mary Pereira worrying over her lover's ghost, his mother desperately but unsuccessfully trying not to think of Nadir; " I am nine years old and lost in the confusion of other people's lives which are blurring together in the heat" (171.)

The first use he makes of his "inner-ear" is to improve his grades at school by reading his teachers' minds as they set the questions, and reading those of the best students' as they write the answers. Perfectly understandable actions and reactions in a nine year old. The adult Saleem, looking back on his early phase, chastises himself for frittering away his talents on inconsequential voyeurism and petty cheating (172).

Saleem next uses his powers to tour India. "But in the end, tourism ceased to satisfy; curiosity began to niggle let's find out [what] . . really goes on around here." He then enters the head of cricketers, film stars and politicians.

When Saleem enters another's head he sees and feels what they see and feel but he apparently cannot *think* what they are thinking.

The next event takes place in February 1957. Saleem, trying to win Evie Burns' attention borrows her bicycle to show-off his expertise, but she is more interested in watching the language-demonstrators parade than in his tricks and he, angry with her, dives into her head, past the language-rioters and pop-songs into her innermost mind where she stands in the doorway of a bedroom holding a bloodstained knife; there is a woman on the bed, and a man enters. At this point, Evie shouts Get Out and pushes him down the slope. "What was it in Evie's head? Crime or dream? I never found out" (192).

Saleem learns from this episode that when he goes really deep into someone's head, they can feel him in there.

On his tenth birthday, Saleem decides to convene a conference of Midnight's Children – his very own M.C.C. – like the cricket M.C.C. that is every boy's dream to play in. However, before their first meeting, Saleem follows his mother to her rendezvous with Nadir Khan. He rides thereafter in her bead as she goes to Nadir's chosen constituency and campaigns for him and his party – the Communist Party of India.

Saleem next launches on getting the M.C.C. together. He enters each of the 580 minds (420 of the original 1001 are dead) and introduces himself, and his purpose – to form "a loose confederation of equals, all points-of-view given equal expression." He runs into trouble with Shiva, who claims he should be the boss because he also was born on the stroke of midnight. Shiva's views are diametrically opposed to Saleem's. Shiva wants a gang, a violent group that would go out "and get what you can, do what you can with it."

The Midnight Children's Conference assembles fairly frequently in the early days of 1958. Saleem wants them to have a purpose. They discuss various possibilities but arrive at no conclusion; Saleem is disappointed that "their heads were full of all the usual things, fathers mothers money food land possessions fame power God" (229).

Saleem decides to keep out of all heads except the children's. Even when he is sent to his Aunt Pia and Uncle Hanif after the hospitalization following the loss of a finger at the school dance he does not use his powers to find out why he had been exiled from home.

But the Children do not hold his interest. They are "a many headed monster, speaking in the myriad tongues of Babel." "They didn't seem very important to me in those days. I had other things in my mind." (252).

The 'other things' are his psychological exile from his parents and his entry into puberty.

Within months of its birth, "the gradual disintegration of the Midnight Children's Conference was already well under way"(254). The time traveller is hurt that no one listens to him; the alchemist is busy using his talent to make his own fortune; the Baud twins have no use for the conference since they are besieged by lovers; more than that, dissensions grow. "Children, however magical, are not immune to their parents," and there were language divisions, economic divisions, regional divisions, and the M.C.C. becomes just another squabbling place. Saleem's broadcasts for unity fall on deaf ears; Shiva capitalizes on this. He is for self-sufficiency in material needs; he scorns Saleem's ideas on brotherhood and argues that each must fight and grab for himself.

Saleem, the narrator, explains at some length that such serious discussion of serious topics is not at all incredible in ten year-olds "in the purer language of thought." That is perfectly understandable, for ten-year-olds, especially chosen ones, can be very intelligent. What is not understandable is that these miracle-children should be so susceptible to parents that they become prejudiced and lose their own identity. Rushdie is drawing an obvious parallel to actual social history where linguistic and economic factions divided India through the 1950s. But in juggling with the two levels – the literal and the metaphorical – Rushdie lets drop the literal ball while he weaves circles with the metaphorical. The Midnight Children who can discuss so intelligently on such topics would also be intelligent enough to realize their uniqueness but they don't. In shifting the blame to parents, Saleem (and Rushdie) is absolving himself (and his generation).

Or, perhaps we should separate Saleem from Rushdie; in such a reading, Rushdie would be making Saleem rationalize on his failure while showing us, the readers, that Saleem (and his generation) is really to blame for his weakness. While this reading would make Rushdie an even better artist, the rest of the novel seems to reinforce the first reading.

Saleem continues to use his powers for petty cheating and inconsequential voyeurism. He finds out more about Lila Sabarmati's affair with Homi Catrack, and in an effort to teach his unfaithful mother a lesson through the other illicit pair, Saleem triggers off a murder and a suicide. Commander Sabarmati shoots Catrack to death and Uncle Hanif, bereft of his source of income, commits suicide.

Then comes Mary Pereira's confession that she had switched babies that eventful midnight; Ahmed and Amina Sinai's real son is Shiva, and Saleem is the son of a street singer, Wee Willie Winkie's wife Vanita, and William Methwold, an Englishman.

This revelation changes Saleem's attitude to Shiva, and the conference; the only way to keep Shiva from penetrating his secret is to refrain from convening a Conference. The Sinais' emigration to Pakistan in October 1958 brings to an end the Midnight Children's Conference, for Saleem's telepathic powers could not penetrate the frontiers of countries. Saleem returns to India for a brief visit in 1962 and then returns permanently in 1971, but for all practical purposes, the Midnight. Children's Conference ceased to be. Nothing, absolutely nothing had been achieved.

But what of the three most talented of the children? Let us consider what happened to them before considering their betrayal of themselves.

Saleem loses his telepathic powers when he undergoes an ear operation in November 1962 but his sense of smell becomes extremely acute. He becomes a citizen of Pakistan, fights in the Pakistan army during its invasion of Bangladesh in 1971, sniffs out Sheikh Mujib, the first President of the new nation, and is then arrested, and meets Parvati-the-witch who helps him escape to India.

They come to Delhi; Saleem marries Parvati, who is pregnant with Shiva's child, on February 23, 1975. The child is born on June 25, 1975, the day Indira Gandhi declared Emergency Rule. Saleem is arrested, tortured into giving the names and identities of all the Midnight Children, and then ectomized of his reproductive organs. And now, in 1978, he writes his autobiography and reads it aloud to Padma, the young woman living with him.

Parvati the witch uses her sorcery to "spirit" Saleem away from Pakistan in a basket. Later she uses her power to call Shiva to her, has his child and dies in the rampage of 1976. All these acts are plainly material though Saleem calls them acts of sorcery.[4]

Shiva, after 1958, reappears in the narrative in 1971 as a war hero, Major Shiva. He leaves a trail of bastard children all over the country, and joins the rampage of 1976 in which the Youth Congress started a City Beautification programme which leveled out slums and drove slum dwellers out of Delhi.

All the Midnight's Children are killed or made impotent in 1976 – but they live on, for Major Shiva, the darkest of them all, had spawned a new generation across the country. Moreover, one could still expect that as a matter of course the 500 odd children would have had two children each by this time when they were in their twenty-ninth year, but Rushdie has ignored this probability.[5]

The stark and gruesome episodes of torture and vasectomies, of eviction slum dwellers and levelling down of slums, the excesses of the nightmare years of the Emergency are all powerfully delineated; and history will show that the truth of those days was far worse than anything portrayed in this novel or elsewhere in literature. But let us consider the deeds of the 1001 Midnight Children within the novel.

The 580 who were alive at the time, as we have seen, did little during the few precious months that they met each other; true, they could not meet after Saleem's departure from India; but they apparently did not do anything on their own either; but we do not know since Saleem never thought of them despite having enough power still left to give their names to his torturers.

But the remaining three, the most gifted three, have been before our eyes long enough for us to know what they did with their powers: Parvati, as we have seen, did little either to help herself or others except for helping Saleem escape; she has the dubious credit of having given birth to an elephant-eared, tubercular son.[6]

We do not see Shiva as having any power other than brute strength, "a force that no one could resist" and he uses this force to enjoy a long line of women and' several military honours. But, let it be said, he never had any altruistic or nationalistic or higher concerns. He carries out his ideology of "Everybody does what I say or I squeeze the shit out of them with my knees" (220).

So Saleem is the worst offender of all. With his telepathic powers, Saleem toured India enjoyed being – a Peeping Tom, improved his grades spied on his mother and aunt, tried unsuccessfully to give a sense of purpose to the Conference, then lost interest blaming his failure on parental indoctrination and the Widow, and then finally betrayed the others to their murderers. With his olfactory powers, he whored all over Karachi reaching a peak of promiscuity with an old crone who could make herself exude the sexual odours of any person she wanted to; he sniffed out Sheikh Mujib and betrayed him to his enemies; he ended up at Mrs. Braganza's pickle factory smelling out the correct proportion of various condiments and ingredients.

It is this treason against himself and his Midnight Children that precludes any final sympathy for Saleem on the reader's part. There is not tragedy, only betrayal.

## Notes

1. Because literary criticism is bound to grow around this novel, I think it is practical to focus sharply on one of the numerous strands and to dispense with all introductory material except for a warning note that what follows is only a part of what can be said about the theme, and an even smaller fraction of what can be said about other aspects of the novel.
2. Salman Rushdie. *Midnight's Children, 1982,* London: Picador (Pan Books) (First published in 1981.*) All* subsequent quotations are from this edition and page references are given in parentheses.
3. Rushdie's interpolation as to the identification of the widow with Mrs Indira Gandhi (421) is in poor taste, and artistically heavy handed.
4. This is one of Rushdie's successful literary techniques. He makes the real appear fantastic and the fantastic appear real (as in the Humming Bird episode) and thus establishes an ambivalence that reinforces the interconnections between the two worlds while appearing to spoof at both.
5. Elsewhere Rushdie has been very careful of plausibility and statistics. For instance, he .has said in an interview published *in Kunapipi* IV:2 1982, that he looked up statistical reports and found that an average of 1,000 babies were being born every hour in the 1940s.
6. Rushdie's choice of names is rather obviously purposeful. "Shiva" and "Parvati" have a son who has elephant ears as in mythology; he is an ailing infant, paralleling India in the first year of Emergency. Padma is repeatedly called "dung lotus" after a colloquial interpolation of a word that has beautiful connotations in Sanskrit. Rushdie is iconoclastic of both Hindu and Muslim beliefs.

# 5

# Salman Rushdie in Indo-English Literature

"Indo-English literature . . . is a bastard child of Britain and a British colony, having, characteristically enough, Christian missionaries as foster parents," I wrote in the opening paragraph of my study of representative Indo-English novelists, published in 1976. This figurative statement is evidently true of the first Indo-English poet, Henry Derozio (1809-1831), whose father was Indian and mother English, and who was inspired by his Indian environment but in diction and style. copied the minor romantics of England His poetic descendants through the nineteenth century and early twentieth – Toru Dutt, Romesh Chunder Dutt, Manmohan Roy wrote in the same vein; it is only with Rabindranath Tagore's poetry and fiction that we see the emergence of a predominantly Indian inspiration and language.

*Midnight's Children* expresses this metaphorical connection in a very literal way – Saleem Sinai, the writer-protagonist, is the son of an Englishman who has seduced the wife of a Hindu street

---

This essay was first published in *The Journal of Indian Writing in English* 12:2 (July 1984) pp. 15-25, and was revised to this version for *The Perforated Sheet* (1988).

singer. He is educated at the Cathedral and. John Connon's Boys' High School in Bombay. He writes an autobiography that in its delineation of boyhood is as poignant as W: O. Mitchell's *Who has seen the Wind,* as authentic as Mark Twain's *Huckleberry Finn,* and as ribald as Roth's *Portnoy's Complaint.* The novel is a landmark in Indo-English literature, and Saleem's parentage is symbolic of his connection to the literature he has enriched. It is interesting to note that the author's biography, in its bare outline, highlights another facet of identity that characterizes this novel – cross-cultural interactions and divided loyalties between Hindus and Muslims, India and Pakistan. Rushdie was born in June 1947 in India and now lives in Britain. His parents emigrated to Pakistan after he left for England.

When asked how he saw himself in relation to other "English speaking Indian writers, people like Mulk Raj Anand, Narayan or Raja Rao," Salman Rushdie's reply was:

> Not at all really. The idea that there is a school of Indian-British fiction is a sort of mistake. Writers like Mulk Raj Anand and Narayan have many more affinities to Indian writers in the Indian languages than they do to a writer like me who just happens to be writing in English.

He felt that except that both he and they use English, they did not have much in common.

Reviewers have already compared him to Garcia Marquez and Gunter Grass for the epic sweep and, political thrust of his imagination. Perhaps one might consider where lie stands in the stream of Indian writing in English although he, like many leading Commonwealth writers, probably dislikes being seen in relation to a 'regional' literature. But *Midnight's Children,* which catapulted him to well-deserved fame in 1981, is the first significant novel in Indo-English literature since Raja Rao's *The Serpent and the Rope* was published in 1960. Both are landmarks in the literary history of Indian writing in English.

His novel *Grimus* is also a rather remarkable piece of writing and is an excellent example of what Rushdie calls the "EnglishEnglish" phase of the colonizing aspect of English literature and language. Had Rushdie not published any novel but in *Grimus,* he would have been an echo of colonial writers in, a post-colonial Commonwealth or a "clever" but minor writer in the contemporary literature of Britain, and one might have agree that Rushdie did not have much in common with other Indo-English writers.

*Grimus is* a fantasy quite unlike anything published in Indo-English literature; a science-fiction story of an earlier intellectual type rather than the blood-and-thunder technological versions popular today. It is a product of a fertile imagination trained in the British educational system common to most erstwhile colonies. For example, there are innumerable literary quotations and historical or philosophical allusions in *Grimus,* and most of them would be familiar to those who have been educated in erstwhile colonies before, say 1960, or in public schools in these countries since then. In that context it is not intellectual but intelligent. The intellectual component is in the conceptualization of the core idea:

> the limitations we place upon the world are composed by ourselves rather than the world. And should we meet things which do not conform to our structure of reality, we place them outside it. Ghosts. Unidentified flying objects. Visions.

There could be another world, or several worlds, right amidst our own, composed of different kinds of solids and empty spaces that could be experienced by perceptual tools different from those that human beings usually have. Grimus has the secret of this inter-dimensional travel and so have the other main characters: Flapping Eagle who is an Amerindian from Axona, Nicholas Deggle and Virgil Beauvoir Chanakya Jones.

Virgil Jones is Flapping Eagle's guide to the Stone Rose which holds the key to the Gate. Jones is, at one point, compared to Sancho and Eagle to Don Quixote; but though the modern picaresque with its share of misadventures and bawdy humour is one dimension of the novel, permeating and surrounding it (to use Jones' words) is another dimension, of philosophical speculation of a world that can be conceptualized and sustained by the power of conceptualization. Grimus' dictum "I think, therefore it exists" is a play on Descartes' "I think, therefore I am," and this word-play is a typical example of the way. Rushdie uses familiar quotations to give a variation to familiar concepts of time, space and reality:

*Grimus* abounds in echoes but Rushdie has no use for echoes per se. He usually uses them for reverberation effects, the original allusion or variation bouncing off against other networks of reference till we are fin an acoustical valley of memory-association reverberations.

Word-play is one of the predominant techniques in the novel. In some cases it is functional. It is understandable that Grimus, the creator of Calf Island and architect behind its ordering, should have assumed a name that is an anagram of Simurg, the all-powerful mythic bird of paradise in Arabic lore, and named the island and mountain 'Calf' after the Arabic letter Kaf which has esoteric connotations. One could stretch the premises of numerology to accept that Liv should be fated to love Grimus who was 54 years old; one could allow for such indulgences as Gorfs being stone frogs who live on the planet Thera lit by Nus that is a sun in the galaxy Yawy Klim (Milky Way); and one could be amused by the farfetched word play in Deggle's leave-taking "Ethiopia," which is a synonym for Abyssinia (I'll be seein' ya); but one is rather perplexed at the function of the Gorfs in the novel. They are an ingenious race, evolved to such a degree that they need no science or art, no job or interest, except the divine Game of Order played according to the rules of Anagrammar.

The Gorfs appear in the novel from time to time but are rather unnecessary to the plot or characterization. There is perhaps a farfetched explanation of their role in the total pattern. Like the question 'Whose dream?' in *Through the Looking Glass,* one might perhaps speculate that Grimus conceptualized Calf Island because Dota the Gorf conceptualized Grimus into existence.

But in its real and pseudo metaphysics, its caravan of characters, its panorama of settings and symbols, there is nothing particularly Indian except for shades of the historical Chanakya that occasionally visits us through Virgil Jones.

But not so with Rushdie's other stories. "The *Free Radio*" is R.K. Narayan first to last. It begins with "We all knew nothing good would happen to him while the thief's widow had her claws dug into his flesh, but the boy was an innocent."

The narrative voice is typically Narayan; the narrator is a retired school teacher ("I am not without importance in the town") who spends his days under a banyan tree at the centre of town, smoking his hookah and keeping his ears open for various tidbits of gossip. This is an ideal narrative voice to comment on a gullible young rickshawallah who is doubly taken in, by a widow with five children who did not want any more, and by an outdated piece of government propaganda that had initially been used to lure men into vasectomization by gifting a radio to each volunteer.

The satire on the government family-planning scheme, and especially on the youths who wore armbands and hustled men into the big white caravan, is very neatly handled. Ramani's naivete and the thief's widow's conniving ways are described in Narayan's vocabulary; and most remarkable of all is the total absence, so characteristic of Narayan and so uncharacteristic of Rushdie, of explicit sexual references.

The style and tone of "The Prophet's Hair" is more that of the Rushdie we hear in *Midnight's Children.* The references are not subtle and the tempo of action is much greater than in the other story. The narrative style seems to have moved towards the traditional Arabic storyteller's. The satire is much sharper. Sheikh Hashim lends money at 71% interest partly "to teach these people the value of money; let them only learn that, and they will be cured of this fever of borrowing." He also, with fatherly concern, guarantees his four sons a secure means of livelihood by smashing their limbs at birth. When they are cured by the beneficence of the Prophet's hair, they are "very properly furious" for the miracle reduced their begging power by 75 %.

The story seems to have been written much earlier than its 1981 publication date. The similes are a little too meticulous: "a winter so fierce it could crack men's bones as if they were glass," "a doorway from which darkness seemed to be pouring like smoke," and a little too frequent; in general, the writing is 'careful' to the point of being strained. It does not flow with the abandon characteristic of *Midnight's Children.*

Placing *Midnight's Children* squarely in the midst of other works of English writing from India is not difficult. Though the rambunctious humour and not-so-clean fun of adolescence reminds one of Tom Jones and Philip Roth's Portnoy, the general pattern of mission school, adolescent sexuality, mother's liaison, sojourn away from home, illegitimate births and initiations bring to mind Manohar Malgonkar's *The Princes*.

Rushdie's experimentation with language is one of his remarkable achievements. Most reviewers have waxed lyrical over this quality. "No Indian novelist has had the courage to handle English language with the gaiety and joyousness of Rushdie," says M. L. Raina; and D. R. Sharma and R Raj Rao, in the same issue of *New Quest*, give numerous examples of Rushdie's marvellous manipulation of English. There is no doubt that Rushdie's mastery of the language is total and that he has 'decolonized' English, perhaps more effectively than the writers he cites in his very significant article in the London *Times* of July 3, 1982. In this article, Rushdie speaks of two waves of decolonizing imposed on English; the first was the wave of American and Irish writers, Joyce and Beckett, Ralph Ellison and James Baldwin, and their contemporaries; the second is the current wave in erstwhile Colonies where English, no longer an English language, grows from many roots; and those whom it once colonized are carving out large territories within the language for themselves.

In this article, Rushdie refers with admiration to G. V. Desani who "showed how English could be bent and kneaded until it spoke in an authentically Indian voice." He includes R. K. Narayan in his list of those who "are busily forging English into new shapes."

Rushdie has not mentioned Raja Rao anywhere in this article, which was published just before a seminar of Indian Writing in English that was held in London early in July 1982 as part of the year-long Festival of India. The omission is interesting because that seminar was, according to some of the participants, a confrontation of the old guard and the new, a turning point when the new guard took over the standard or banner. Whether it is right to make categories according to age rather than literary characteristics, and thereby place together such writers as Nirad

Chaudhuri and Raja Rao on one side, and Salman Rushdie, Anita Desai and Sasti Brata on the other is a relevant question. However, according to reports, there was a heated debate at a panel discussion at which all these writers were present.

Whether the two writers like it or not, there are certain similarities between *The Serpent and the Rope* and *Midnight's Children*. Both are landmarks in Indo-English literature. Both give an authentic delineation of Indian life and attitudes, and if they are dissimilar they are so because of the diversity of India. The charge that Raja Rao's Brahmin-Sanskrit oriented ethos gives a one-sided picture of India is only as valid as saying that a novel with a Muslim as protagonist cannot be representative of Indian life or values. In both, the narrative gets lost in a flood of material; a torrent of metaphysical ideas in the earlier novel and, a flood of tangential socialite events and irrelevant politics in the later novel.

Ruth Prawer Jhabwala's statement on the ideal Indian novel would apply to both:

> . . . . bits of prose-poetry, anecdotes, lots of philosophizing and musing, and oblique kinds of wit, and ultimate self surrender, a sinking back into formlessness.

Moreover, both writers have consciously and conscientiously experimented with language. Consciously, as seen in Raja Rao's now-familiar preface *to Kanthapura* where he says we cannot write like the English and we should not, and looks "forward to a time when the Indian dialect of English becomes as rich and distinctive as its Irish or American counterpart." Written in 1938, this preface uses exactly the same examples as Rushdie uses in the July 1982 article cited above.

Both have succeeded eminently in their experimentation and innovations regarding language. The diction they use in each story is perfectly suited to the narrative voice which in turn is well suited to the story being narrated; the leisurely pace of the old village woman in *Kanthapura* uses an idiom that is drawn from the local Kannada background and shaped by puranic tales and practical everyday chores. Govindan Nair's phrases and attitude in *The Cat and Shakespeare* are very authentic, as is Rama's intellectual and anguished voice in *The Serpent and the Rope.* So also with Rushdie's narrative voice. In *Midnight's Children,* the vocabulary given to each character rings true: the mission-school student's, "Hey, what're you up to, man? You running away from home secretly and all?" Major Latif's Sandhurst-jargon and club-superficiality, "I just rub my jolly old lamp, and out pops the genie bringing fame and fortune. Your girl will be in darn, good hands. *Darn good";* and Tai Bibi's vernacular idioms: "Hey, Bhaenchud.! Hey, little sister-sleeper, where you running?"; Mrs. Braganza's "there's nothing but dirt in the heads of the mens."

Two of the most challenging aspects of verisimilitude in language are the problems of conveying the flavour of the idiom and of making clear what language is being spoken by the character at any given time. Both Raja Rao and Rushdie succeed in the first challenge. Mulk Raj Anand is, of course, the one who started exploring the potential in literal-translations of vernacular idioms. But Raja Rao and Rushdie have more variations of class and imagery because their dramatis personae are drawn from a wider range of society. Rama's metaphors, for example, are usually drawn from the *Upanishads* and Achakka's from the *Puranas;* a variation that reflects their backgrounds, and Raja Rao's craftsmanship. Similarly with Rushdie. He has an even wider span of social classes, more subtle shades of class-hierarchies, and the distinctions between Mary Pereira's Goanese-English and the boys' school-language are brought out well.

The second challenge, of distinguishing between those who speak English and those who do not is more difficult. Mulk Raj Anand and Raja Rao do not have this problem. It is clear that no one in *Kanthapura* speaks in English except for an occasional, clearly identified sentence or two. In *The Serpent and the Rope* some characters speak in English, some in French, some in Kannada; but the distinctions are clear or, immaterial. In R. K. Narayan the distinctions are immaterial. Everyone speaks, or understands, a mixture of Indian-English and the vernacular; more relevant, in Narayan, *what* is said is important but seldom is the imagery or diction used by characters of particular significance.

In *Midnight's Children,* these aspects are important. The vocabulary used by a character is part of the characterization.

Also, it is necessary to consider the correlation between the language used by the character and Rushdie's transcription of it.

English, Hindi and Urdu seem to be the three main languages used by the characters. This might seem like mere hair-splitting, and certainly in the context of Rushdie's prodigious achievement it is a small aspect; but if one were to conclude that Padma does not speak in English, we have a problem. Her hallmark interjection, "Mister" is easily explained, for that is commonly used all over India, no matter what the language. Even her imperatives and inversion of statement to question (e.g. "Why you're waiting? Begin, Begin all over again." [347]) are explainable as translations that retain the flavour of the vernacular. But what happens to words like the much-quoted "writery" or "looker-after" or the even more difficult "writing-shiting" whose word-play depends on the specificities of the English language?

Padma is a very intriguing narrative device and a marvellous character in her own right. She is also a symbol of India, of contact with the earth that an artist needs to be an artist, of that anchor of sanity that keeps Saleem sane. She is many things within the novel and certainly deserves a full length study. However, within this context, it is interesting, indeed ironic, that she should be so much the idealized feminine stereotype that we find in Raja Rao's novels. Padma and Little Mother *(The Serpent and the Rope)* are, at first sight, as dramatically opposed a pair as one could think of. Padma is earthy, loud-mouthed, ever eager to get Saleem's "other pencil" to work; Little Mother is saintly, silent and chaste. But, both have the traditional womanly virtues of seeing themselves as the givers of selfless service to their man, as receivers of the seed of life; they see loyalty and love-making as of prime importance, so that their sacrifice of the latter for the former becomes a supreme one.

> (For) a woman her womb is her life, and we cannot choose our men. (*Serpent and the Rope*)

> What creatures we are, we women, never for one moment at peace when our men lie sick and low . . . . This love, mister, it will drive a women to craziness. (*MNC.* p. 192)

Feminists might shudder at this chauvinism but traditionalists would laud the idealization that lies at the root of such an attitude.

Rushdie's women-characters are varied; but none, not even Reverend Mother with her regal mass and mustache, rebels at the traditional role of the male as the ultimate authority in a household. On the other hand, most of the male characters are weak (it is, not only Saleem who, has, to say, "women have made me; and also unmade,") whereas most of the women are strong and independent. They invariably get what they want because they have the strength or willpower; the force is with them, so to say, and they know how to reach their goal: by silence and feminine cajoling as with Amina inducing herself to fall in love with her husband; by ambitious drive as with Emerald; by preternatural willpower (?) as with Jamila who holds her body from entering puberty so that her marriage to a. weakling need never be consummated. And then there is Padma, who does not have to resort to any wiles of perforated bedsheet or Pioneer Cafes but takes matters into her own hands, herself proposing marriage "so that I can look after you without going to shame in the eyes of the world."

Rushdie may not believe there exists an Indo-English stream of literature or that he is part of it, but literary historians would have to disagree.

# 6

# The Perforated Sheet

## Method as Meaning in *Midnight's Children*

> I had an enormous typescript, probably a thousand pages, which was completely undisciplined. But, out of that, I found myself putting the story into the first person, as a way of controlling what was otherwise a mess of material.
>
> (*Kunapipi,* IV: 2, 1982)

> The meaning of the *leitmotif is* the sum total of the incidents in which it occurs . . . . And what one is able to do by using the leitmotif is to orchestrate what would otherwise be a huge mass of material, which doesn't always have rational connections, but the, leitmotif can provide this other network of connections and so provide a shape.
>
> (*Kunapipi,* VII: 1, 1985)

Salman Rushdie's *Midnight's Children* is certainly not a tightly structured novel but it is held together by a scaffolding of images, metaphors, and other narrative devices. Despite the seeming chaos of narration, there is an architectural balance that a literary draughtsman can easily discern even though there are

---

This was Chapter 5 of my earlier work, *The Perforated Sheet: Essays on Salman Rushdie's Art.*

many extensive underground chambers which can be reached only through trapdoors in the floor, which are covered by carpets and mats as in Aadam's Agra house. The literary devices that Rushdie uses are ingenious and one watches spell-bound as one does a magician's performance even when one knows about mirrors and false-bottomed boxes. Because the structure is so sprawling, Rushdie has posted maps at various points, complete with floor-pattern and "You are here" signs. There are periodical summaries of events that have happened (e.g. p. 237) and condensed reviews from time to time of events and people yet to come. Then there ate picture windows to which he takes the reader for panoramic views of the historical landscape. There are recurring motifs and murals that are like melodic refrains in a symphony. And then there are gargoyles – scatological or pornographic interlude – a few of which are functional and others gratuitous. All in all, certainly not an edifice of stream-lined functionalism but a rambling rococo manor-house.

Recurring images and metaphors have an important function in Rushdie's method and meaning. The perforated sheet is one of the basic metaphors.

Dr. Aadam Aziz, newly returned from Heidelberg to his native Srinagar, – falls in love with Naseem Ghani, whose various illnesses he diagnoses through a seven-inch hole in a bed-sheet held in front of her afflicted part by two of her three "musculatured" maids. Over a period of three, years he sees all parts of her body, culminating in a sight of her face "on the day the [first] World War ended".

There are a number of cues and clues given in this incident, one of the first of the countless incidents that make up *Midnight's Children*.

One, the idea of holding a perforated sheet for a doctor's diagnostic examination seems "fantastic" in a literary and literal sense of the word, but it is just an *exaggeration of the real* purdah that is part of Muslim culture. This is a point that readers, especially those unfamiliar with the cultural milieu of Rushdie's Asian novels, should bear in mind. Even the preternatural powers of Midnight's children are little more than a compilation of news stories that would appear over any three-year period in a regional newspaper. Establishing a willing suspension of disbelief within an Indian cultural milieu is very easy.

Two, there are numerous "cultural" reference, some of which work as symbols. In an Indian wedding, Hindu and Muslim, there is a point at which the bridal couple take their "first look" at each other. This happens when a screen – of silk or cloth or straw or whatever – held between the couple by two relatives is drawn away; or when the bride's veil is lifted and her face appears recessed in what would effectively be a seven-inch hole in the richly sequined veil draped over the bride's head and shoulders like a cowl. (Nadir, for example, lifts Amina's veil, *MNC*, 57) Having Aadam see Naseem through a perforated sheet is parodic of the custom of purdah and also a foreshadowing of their marriage. Yet another cultural overtone in this incident is that though the formal proposal among Muslims has to come from the bridegroom's family, all the strategies and ploys that engineer the move are set in place by the bride's family; here again, Rushdie parodies the elaborate protocol of marriage negotiations.

Three, one of the structural devices in *Midnight's Children* is that of linking Saleem's family history with the history of India, and occasionally, as here, of the world. Saleem says, after referring to Naseem's headache on the day the – World War ended, "Such historical coincidences have littered and perhaps befouled my family's existence in the World." *(MNC, 27)*. 'Rushdie has said in lectures that a child thinks of the world as revolving around itself because of the attention he gets from everyone around. Saleem never outgrows this childhood perception; indeed, Rushdie draws it to an extreme as when Saleem says:

> it is my firm conviction that the hidden purpose of the Indo-Pakistani war of 1965 was nothing more nor less than the elimination of my benighted family from the face of the earth. (*MNC*, 338)

Again, Saleem is representative of his generation, indeed, of all Indians:

> I am everyone everything whose being-in-the-world affected was affected by mine . . . . Nor am I particularly exceptional in this matter; each "I", everyone of, the now-six-hundred-million-plus of us, contains a similar multitude. *(MNC,* 383)

Four, the historical events mentioned usually have a reflection-connection with the course of personal events. Aadam's courtship (1915-1918) coincides largely with the span of the first world war (1914-1918); with the end of the war, the world looked forward to an era of peace and return to family bonds; similarly, Aadam looked forward to a life of conjugal felicity. That things turned out otherwise for the couple could be taken as Rushdie's comment on the aftermath of the world war; more likely, however, it is one of Rushdie's usual inversions that people might get married but seldom live happily ever after. The day the world war ended was, in other words, the beginning "of frequent and devastating warfare" between Aadam and Naseem.

Finally, the perforated sheet goes far beyond its literal context. It accumulates weight with repeated use; it becomes symbolic of the passage of time in the way it gets moth-eaten, and of lack of unity within India in the way it develops numerous holes; by cross-reference it is associated with-Pakistan "that moth-nibbled land of God"; the way the sheet is stored as a. sentimental souvenir reflects an attitude to history, the attitude that treasures something long after it has become useless; or it could be a comment on the new generation's ignorance of history or their callousness in letting it get moth-eaten. It also becomes a lesson in how to fall in love. Amina Sinai, married to Ahmed but still in love with her impotent first husband Nadir, trains herself to love Ahmed.

> To do this she divided him, mentally, into every single one of his component parts. Each day she selected one fragment of Ahmed Sinai, and concentrated her entire being upon it . . . until she felt fondness rising up within her and becoming affection, and, finally, love. (*MNC,* 68)

What Aadam Aziz had done because he had no option in the purdah culture, Amina does with purposeful concentration. History repeats itself but in more ways than one, as happens to

Amina: her second husband becomes as impotent as her first after their second child.

The perforated sheet in the context of love appears again when Mutanm falls in love "head-over-heels with the glimpses of her [Jamila's] demure eyes he saw through her perforated sheet." (*MNC*, 321).

Finally, the perforated sheet is the metaphor for both method and message. "There are so many stories to tell" (*MNC* 9) that Saleem (and Rushdie) cannot use a linear narrative. Instead, they use Lifafa Das's peepshow method, showing successive scenes through a hole; one can show close-ups and long shots in a seemingly irrational sequence but the cumulative effect, as with the peepshow, is that one has seen all of life. "See the whole world, come see everything!" (*MNC*, 75). The metaphor also conveys Saleem's and Rushdie's message that nothing can be seen, experienced or communicated in its entirety, or shown either. Those who try to see or show "everything" come to grief; as did Uncle Hanif with his dream of writing the perfect script for the perfect movie or his persistent bid to collect all thirteen hearts while playing rummy, and Lifafa Das who tried to "deliver what he promised" and loaded his bioscope machine with picture postcards of Monuments, natural and manmade disasters, politicians, pavement-dwellers, semi nudes, in no particular sequence. In the end it all adds up to the total picture. Or as often "it all blows up in one's face."

Another related image is in baby Saleem's initial refusal to blink. This is a foreshadowing of his desire to encompass everything. But he learns soon enough. "The first lesson of my life: nobody can face the world with his eyes open all the time." (*MNC*, 125) In this context, the perforated sheet is like the eyelids; or in a Biblical analogy, the burning bush or the cloud above Sinai that shields the eyes from seeing too much reality.

Another reason why Rushdie never completely removes the perforated sheet between himself and his 'reader is because "the young girl behind the sheet and the gauche young Doctor turned rapidly into different, stranger beings" (*MNC*, 34) once the perforated sheet is drawn away from between them. In his characterizations, he thus justifies his gaps and jumps. If we see any inconsistency between the landowner's daughter, who schemingly seduced the young doctor by baring small parts of her body, and the new bride, who is shocked when told to move like a woman *(MNC,* 33), we keep our questions to ourselves for we see the larger consistency of her entirely credible growth into Reverend Mother, "mustachioed; matriarchal, proud" as she sits "in her glass confessional and solved the problems of the world "(*MNC,* 328).

Rushdie leaves a trail of direct and indirect references to the perforated sheet. Both Saleem and Aadam are identified figuratively with the sheet. Aadam has a hole in the core of his being, Saleem too is perforated. He feels "condemned by a perforated sheet to a life of fragments" *(MNC* 121). Castrated, lobotomized, sperectomized, Saleem is a perforated sheet held together by Padma's devoted nursing and his will to complete his narrative.

The perforated sheet is related through a loose network of associations to various other events and characters as well. Lifafa Das's peep-show machine also is a device where one looks through a hole, and peep-shows are another medium for voyeurs. Saleem becomes a voyeur through his telepathic power. Tai Bibi provides him with another kind of voyeurism through olfactory powers and he enjoys and suffers a third kind of voyeurism through his own sniffing abilities.

Holes, bodily orifices in particular, hold a fascination for Saleem-Rushdie and there are endless references to these holes and what comes out of them. References to Saleem's nasal orifice become quite nauseating with repetition. As with Mordecai Richler's numerous synonyms in *Cocksure, Midnight's Children* provides a compenditun of colloquialisms for penis. Rushdie and his native Urdu language make for a more colourful list than Richler's.

Where there's a hole, there's likely to be some leaking. Images of leaking build up another major, metaphor for Rushdie's narrative method and his message about interconnections. Things flow into as well as out of Saleem. He is "a swallower of lives." Stories wait in him as dynasties waited in Aadam's nose.

> Most of what matters in our lives takes place in our absence: but I seem to – have found from somewhere the trick of

> filling in the gaps in my knowledge, so that everything is in my head, down to the last detail . . . . (*MNC*, 19)

Imagination leaks on to memory, filling gaps, and then Saleem leaks them on to paper. Basically, this describes the process of writing. A writer, like Reverend Mother in her glass confessional, hears about (swallows) others' lives. He fills in the gaps with his imagination and then writes down the stories, not always in any logical sequences. The reader inverts the process, sees fragmented episodes, fills them out with his imagination and figures out the beauty of the naked woman, behind the perforated sheet.

Things flow into and out of Saleem but there is a difference in the rate of flow. The inflow is torrential, whereas the outflow is a leak. Saleem is "a swallower of lives"; "multitudes are flooding" into him *(MNC*, 126*)*.

Things leak out of Saleem. Other "manly men," as Chaucer would say, receive and give with greater force. To them "truth comes in blows" as Saul Bellow's oversize overloud Henderson the Rain King would say. Aadam was hit on the nose by a tussock of earth "gloved in a prayer mat" (*MNC*, 11) a Ahmed Sinai, in bed with his wife, relives being slapped in the face by a "barely chewed Parsec hand" dropped by a vulture flying from the Towers of Silence (*MNC* 91); Joseph. D'Costa, Uncle, Hanif, Mutasim the Handsome, even poor, scared Zafar feel truth coming in blows; Saleem's entire family is wiped out in an explosion that destroyed their "Rawalpindi bungalow, perforated sheets at whose centre hung a mysterious dark hole." *(MNC*, 342).

Truth comes in blows to Saleem too, we must grant. Tony Catrack's nudge is the first blow; the washing-chest escapade the second; and being hit by the silver spittoon the third. There were other blows dealt by the Widow. However, an impression of his passivity is established so strongly at the beginning that we are made to feel that "leaking" is just the right word for Saleem. One of the first details we are given about him is that he his trouble doing even that. His impotence is both physical and, literary. Padma, who manages to remove his literary block fails in the other matter even when she puts her left foot on my right, winds her right leg around my waist, inclines her head up toward mine and makes cooing noises . . (*MNC*, 39).

The first reference to leaking occurs in the third chapter:

> Things-even people-have a way of leaking into each other . . . like flavours when you cook . . . the past has dripped into me . . . . So we can't ignore it. (*MNC*, 38)

This passage encapsulates several of Rushdie's messages: the influence of personal and public history on individuals; the interrelatedness of people in the context of Saleem-as-Everyman; and the interrelatedness of past and present in any culture. It also defines Rushdie's method whereby he defies the one-book-one-hero narrative tradition and justifies having a novel made up entirely of numerous minor characters and, subplots.

Though Saleem has his own identity, he is the sum total of all that has flooded and leaked into him as well as his own original components. The chapter "Tick, tock" provides a summary of what has gone before, all that has seeped into Saleem. The device very successfully integrates the personal ands national experiences and thereby expresses the message that Saleem is every Indian – and that every Indian is part of India's history just as India's history is part of every Indian's blood-stream.

> I move on, acquiring Mahatma Gandhi and his hartal...swallowing the moment at which Aadam Aziz did not know whether he was Kashmiri or Indian . . . . and I'm gulping down Dyer; moustache and all. I'm getting heavier by the second, fattening up on washing chests...aunt runs traitorously through Agra . . . . and that feeds me too . . . . (*MNC*, 107-108)

Thus, the leaking comes from everywhere, not just from those personally and immediately around him: Methwold's centre parting secret that "has dripped down" (102) and Amina's assiduity that has seeped in (108) and Mary Pereira's Blue Jesus that leaked in (109). Saleem becomes an amorphous sponge, the same way as Reverend Mother in her glass booth.

Or perhaps he is closer to Amino in one of her phases where people open up to her. Sometime before Saleem's washing-chest escapade, Amina is guilt ridden for past lapses.

> Amina had become one of those rare people who take the burdens of the world on their own backs; she began to exude the magnetism of the willingly guilty; and from then on everyone who came into contact with her felt the most powerful of urges to confess their own, private guilts ....when my uncle Hanif and his wife the divine Pia came to call they related their quarrels in minute detail; Lila Sabarmati confided her infidelities . . . . (*MNC*, 158)

Like Amina, Saleem feels with and for his whole generation. He feels directly responsible for Midnight's Children and his guilt is more justified than Amina's considering how he had betrayed their names to the government. For him, writing his story is like penance, an atonement for his past lapses which he feels has been his whole life.

The past cannot be ignored. Indeed, it has to be preserved Saleem certainly thinks so, arid and hence his feverish haste to complete his record. . He feels that soon he will

> crumble into (approximately) six hundred and thirty million particles (the population of India) of anonymous, and necessarily oblivious dust. This is why I have resolved to confide in paper, before I forget. (We are a nation of forgetters.) (*MNC*, 37)

One of his reasons for writing is that his son "needed to know my story" (*MNC*, 211). If Aadam were his father's son, he would find out the story for himself, as Saleem found out about Aadam Sr. But Saleem feels impelled to write it down because he feels that Aadam, despite having ears that resemble Ganesha's, will not have the wisdom of that god because the natural process of evolution in society and politics has suffered so seriously that there are mutations, and a risk that collective memory itself might be lost. Saleem has to leave a record.

Preservation or recording, as *a* function of literature is another message that uses its, own medium as method.

The narrator of *Shame* at one point says: "I, too, face the problem of history: what to retain; what-to dump, how to hold on to what memory insists on relinquishing. (S, 87)"

As though to circumvent this problem of selection, Saleem seemingly retains everything. His device of linking personal landmarks with national landmarks. provides him with a peg on which to hang relevant historical data. In addition, he throws in a lot of gratuitous information borrowed right out of reference books. A typical example would be the string of statistics attached to Saleem's announcement of his tenth birthday"

> although the production of finished steel reached only 2.4 million tons by the plan's end in 1961...the production of iron ore was almost doubled; power capacity did double; coal production leaped from thirty-eight million to fifty-four million tons. Five billion yards of cotton textiles were produced each year. *(MNC,* 206).

He goes on to add that the literacy rate had not gone up. But if this is satire, it does not hit its mark. The satire comes through, though, in other instances, as when Rushdie lists the dangerous promises made by candidates during the election campaigns of 1957:

> the Jan Sangh was campaigning for rest homes for aged sacred cows; in Kerala, E.M.S. Namboodiripad was promising that Communism would give everyone food and jobs; in Madras, the Anna-DMK party of C.N. Annadurai fanned the flames of regionalism; the Congress fought back with reforms such as the Hindu Succession Act which gave Hindu women equal rights of inheritance .... (*MNC*, 185)

The list above has little. to do with Saleem but Rushdie ingeniously links it with his present predicament of wooing Evie Burns; while each party – was campaigning for its own cause, Saleem requests Sonny to campaign on his behalf.

Incidentally, it is interesting to note that Rushdie uses the real names of politicians in *Midnight's Children* whereas he does not identify the politicians explicitly in *Shame*. One of the – reasons could be that politicians such as Harappa-Bhutto and Hyder-Zia are main characters in *Shame* whereas they are not even peripheral characters in *Midnight's Children*. Another reason could be that Rushdie has learnt how to use political figures; that he has matured in this area between the two novels. The listing of information is very heavy-handed towards the end of the chapter, "A Wedding ", where Saleem parallels the thirteen days of Parvati's labour to the thirteen days that preceded the proclamation of Emergency Rule in June, 1975.

The chronicle on Mrs. Gandhi at the very end of that chapter (*MNC*, 421) is not only in bad taste [irrespective of the later assassination] but also negates by its explicitness much of the cutting edge of the political satire.

Like Lifafa Das (whose name literally means 'envelope' and idiomatically means "empty show") Rushdie keeps adding facts, figures, opinions. Satire is never far from any page; readers of. Rushdie's generation or its preceding one would have their recollections nudged to life on every page. But not everything is historical. Rushdie's focus is on the power of memory and, not on historicity, this despite his recognition that memory can be deceptive.

Saleem realizes two errors of historical dates in his writing – that the elections of 1957 actually took place before his tenth birthday which inaugurated his telepathic conference – and therefore he could not have known anything about Shiva's Cowboys tampering with ballot boxes, as he had first claimed (*MNC*, 222); and that he had got Mahatma Gandhi assassinated at the wrong part of the narrative (*MNC*, 166 and 142).

Of this, Rushdie has said that he realized the deceptiveness of memory when he remembered "very clearly his own reaction and that of the general public to the declaration of the Indo-Chinese war of 1962 when as a matter of fact he had been at school in England.

> That showed me that memory does play very extraordinary tricks on you. So that's why I made Saleem make that kind of mistake . . . . I found that I did not have total recall of the past, that I was remembering certain things very vividly, sometimes accurately and sometimes not. (Kunapipi, IV, 2, 1982)

Whether Saleem's errors were purposely put in there or were allowed to stay there and then rationalized, the point that Rushdie was making in the interview was that if one sees history through something – object, event or person – dear to oneself, it becomes distorted. I would say, though, that some essential truth often emerges from some of the distortions. The novel itself exemplifies this. Its historicity, or lack thereof, is not of any importance whereas the understanding it generates of the post-Independence generation is significant.

In this context, we could consider what Rushdie has said in the novel about the distinction between reality and truth.

> What's real and what's true aren't necessarily the same. . . True was a thing concealed just over the horizon.*(MNC, 79)*

> Reality is a question of perspective; the further you get from the past, the more concrete, and plausible it seems but as you approach the present, it inevitably seems more and more incredible. (*MNC*, 165)

> Sometimes legends make reality, and become more useful than facts. *(MNC, 47)*

> Reality can have metaphorical content; that does not make it less real. . . Midnight's children can be made to represent many things, according to your point of view . . . . but what they must not become is the bizarre creation of a rambling, diseased mind. (*MNC*, 200)

> In all literature, what actually happened is less important that what the author can manage to persuade his audience to believe. *(MNC, 271)*

The most important of these quotations explicitly gives Rushdie's rationale regarding his method and his objective:

> I told you the truth....Memory's truth, because memory has its own special kind. It selects, eliminates, alters, exaggerates, minimizes, glorifies, and vilifies also; *but in the end, it creates its own reality, its heterogeneous but usually coherent version of events;* and no sane human being ever trusts someone else's version more than his own. *(MNC,* 211, italics mine).

The italicized statement is a brilliant summation of what Saleem and Rushdie have succeeded in doing. The last part, however, is one of those unfortunate reversals that questions the usefulness of the preceding process. If each one has to find his own version, what is the point in Saleem's mad rush to write everything, down?

> In justifying his own stance, Saleem is negating what he has just said little earlier
>
> My son will understand. As much as for any living being, I'm telling my story for him, so that afterwards, when I've lost my struggle against cracks, he will know.... (*MNC* 211).

Saleem's record holds some: essential truths; not the whole Truth with a capital T, but enough truths to be of interest and relevance to his son and ensuing generations; and sane people must trust Saleem's version if they are to avoid the tragedy of his betrayal of his country and his country's betrayal of him.

Saleem's chronicle is worth preserving; and Rushdie drives this message home with the metaphor of pickling, which is the most consistently developed metaphor next to that of the perforated sheet. There is a carefully built circularity of structure: Mary Pereira's pickles and chutneys are a culinary treat in the Sinai household in their days of affluence. One of Uncle Hanif's dreams is to shoot a film "of a pickle-factory created, run and worked in entirely by women" (*MNC*, 244); towards the end of Saleem's story, which is the beginning of Rushdie's novel, he is taken under wing by Padma, a worker in a. pickle-factory created, run and worked in by women, and its owner is Mary Pereira, now known as Mrs. Braganza.

Saleem makes the connection between different parts of the metaphor quite explicitly early in the novel:

> And my chutneys and kasaundies are, after all, connected to my nocturnal scribblings – by day amongst the pickle-vats, by night within these sheets, I spend my time at the great work of: preserving. Memory, as well as fruit, is being saved from the corruption of the clocks. (*MNC*, 38).

There are several other dimensions to the way the metaphor of pickling acts both as method and meaning.

Pickles add taste to a meal, and spice to life. Pickles *change* the original form of the fruit or vegetable used, apropos of how the narrative "makes reality and becomes more useful than facts." A number of condiments are thrown into the pickle-vats. The smell and taste of oil and ground mustard (vinegar in Rushdie's recipe) are so overpowering, one might wonder about the need for other condiments, but no pickle-maker would omit any of them, for in the end, it creates its own reality, its heterogeneous but usually coherent version.

But chutneys are somewhat different. Like pickles, they add taste to a meal and have a variety of ingredients but they change the original form *completely*. They do not just stir and boil and mix; in chutneys the ingredients are pound, ground, pulverized – words and processes that are very, appropriate for what happens to Saleem.

A common idiom of threat is to say "I'll make chutney of you."(which term goes somewhat farther than its equivalent "mincemeat"). The phrase is very appropriate to Saleem's gruesome description of the sterilization programme imposed during the Emergency; the metaphor, by extension, applies to India's strength and creativity, just as the cracks that Saleem "claims to have are symbolic of the many cracks in the edifice of national unity.

Rushdie ends his novel with a reference to pickles in the latter, negative sense. He picks up the jar reference connected with Saleem's birth. Saleem's (or was it Shiva's) umbilical cord, floating in a pickle (sterilized of course) jar of salted water. Now he reiterates the metaphor:

> Symbolic value of the pickling process: all the six hundred million eggs which gave birth to the population of India could fit inside a single standard-sized pickle jar. ...every pickle jar ... contains, therefore the most exalted of possibilities, the feasibility of the chutnification of history, the grand hope of the pickling of time! I, however, have pickled chapters...in words and pickles, I have immortalized my

> memories, have pickled, although distortions are inevitable in both methods. (*MNC*, 459)

Rushdie's method is analogous to pickling, his meaning to chutney.

In addition to metaphors, Rushdie uses other leitmotifs to "orchestrate" his material. The main refrains are the two prophecies that accompany Saleem's birth: the private one that is addressed to Saleem the individual by Ramram Seth and the public prophecy addressed to Saleem, child of Independence by Prime Minister Jawaharlal Nehru. These have been discussed elsewhere in this volume. What has not been mentioned is that this device has Biblical associations, echoing such Biblical phrases as "As had been foretold" or "that it might be fulfilled."

Padma provides yet another important metaphor. Her relationship to Saleem is that of reader to writer, audience 'to actor. An analysis of this relationship must wait its time; meanwhile, it might be mentioned that the appellation, "Dung-Goddess" for goddess Lakshmi is one of those "distortions" that Saleem says are inevitable in the kind of narrative he has undertaken. Padma "the Lotus calyx" as he says (*MNC*, 194) is of the lotus and the lotus is a flower that grows in the shallow, muddy shores of ponds and rivers. Mud, slush, slime, muck, mire, bog, swamp; any of these would be acceptable, for they have more than one meaning, and one of the meanings is the kind of swampy mud in which the lotus grows. But "dung" has only one meaning and that very definitely has nothing to do with the lotus or goddess Lakshmi, one of whose names is Padma.

Rushdie's use of the phrase "Dung-goddess" then, is one of: his misfired efforts at making dramatic connections. "Earth" or "mind" are not dramatic, but "dung" is.

Rushdie's propensity to manipulate dramatic ironies is far more successful in the matter of noses. Saleem's Cyranose is a leitmotif that is marvellously handled to mislead without any cheating on the writer's part. Starting off with Aadam Aziz' nose which is described at length, (*MNC*, 13), Rushdie like a good detective-novelist also lets drop that Methwold had such a nose too. Rushdie squeezes dry almost every denotation and connotation of words phrases and idioms associated with nose. Saleem makes a living by his nose sniffing out people and then the correct combinations of pickling ingredients for his living. He has a nose for details, pokes his nose into others' affairs . . . . There is an advertisement for facial-tissues that runs "No one knows noses like we know noses." They have not heard of Salman Rushdie, obviously.

## Note

1. This is a word-sketch of one of the better known poses of the *Kama Sutra* and Khajuraho erotica. It is curious that Rushdie uses almost the same words and pose in the opening paragraph of Chapter Forty-Two of *Grimus*.

# 7

# New Dimensions Courtesy of the Whirling Demons

## Word-Play in *Grimus*

> The structure of a novel and whatever it communicates are under the direct control of the novelist's manipulation of language, and concomitantly, of the reader's re-creative sympathy, his desire and ability to realize and release the technique from the verbal clues deposited by the author.
>
> Roger Fowler[1]

Roger Fowler in a brilliant exposition of his critical theory, develops the idea that the structure of a novel is analogous to the structure of a sentence; as in a sentence, there are syntactic (superficial) and semantic (deep) elements, and two levels – *histoire* (story) and discourse (language).

In *Grimus*, the narrative and the structure, the superficial and deeper themes, are ingeniously interconnected through what the Gorfs in the novel call "Ordering."

---

This essay appeared in *Reading Rushdie: Perspectives on the fiction of Salman Rushdie*. Edited By D.M. Fletcher. Amsterdam: Rodopi. 1993. pp. 35-43.

> "Talent" to the Gorfs means only one thing: skill at Ordering. Thus the very skill that caused the Chiefest Question to be asked must be used in its solution, with the aid of the "Learninglobe," that inexhaustible memory-vault locked within each Gorf, giving the species absolute recall of anything that has ever befallen any Gorf.[2]

The ability to realize and release verbal clues deposited by the author makes *Grimus* a fascinating game for a Gorf-reader. Rushdie builds a rather elaborate narrative edifice and as a Gorf-writer he is careful to have at instant recall all the data and clues he has earlier put into the narrative, so that he can reinforce some of his points. The Gorf-reader can unlock the puzzle because he shares the same Endimion as the Gorf-writer and therefore has the power of absolute recall of *anything that has ever befallen any* Gorf. The Endimion shared by the reader and writer in this context is the world of literary allusions and word-play.

The narrative is reinforced at every step with a network of allusions. The plot is centred on the concretization of an ingenious concept. In the World as we know it, people exist *concurrently* in different *spaces* – all over the world, for example. But it could be that there is a world where the spatial dimension is the same but the time dimension as different, as would be the case if different pages of a city's history were presented at the same time. Or, there could be a time-space continuum parallel to our own, concurrent and conspatial but separated by the limitation of our senses. Rushdie calls these worlds Dimensions.

> Here we all are, a world of living beings and inanimate objects and gusts of breeze, all of us composed of infinitely more empty space than solid matter. Is it not a conceptual possibility that here, in our midst, permeating all of us and all that surrounds us, is a completely other world, composed of different kinds of solids, different kinds of empty spaces, with different perceptual tools which make us as nonexistent to its inhabitants as they are to ours? In a word, another dimension. *(Grimus,* 55/52)

The action combines imaginative flights of science fiction, extravagance of fantasy, and clever twists of sexual humour typical of Rushdie.

The element of fantasy is very strong in all of Rushdie's work. Some essential components of fantasy are disorientation in time, dislocation in space, distortion of actuality, and what Anders in his study of Kafka calls "the literal metaphor."[3] In *Grimus,* all these characteristics are at an obvious level, without going into psychological or political dimensions.

The novel starts in time present and develops as a literal reading of Eliot's concept of time past and time future being contained in time present. Eagle starts out from Axona Plateau in our century, as seen in his brief trip to the plain on his twenty-first birthday; he wanders for 700 years, presumably in the past, and is flung ashore on Calf Island, presumably in our not-too-distant future. But all of this could be concurrent with the present in another dimension. So also with space. Axona Plateau is somewhere in America but Calf Island is in another dimension, and at the end Eagle and Media presumably return to the world as we know it.

One of the most important points about fantasy is that it cannot work except with actuality as the springboard, which is what I mean when I say that "distortion of reality" is an essential component. If the correlative of the familiar is totally abstracted there are no points of reference; and the unfamiliar cannot exist in a vacuum: it gains its existence only through the familiar. In other words, literature and experience are relevant to man only insofar as they come within the orbit of his perceptions. The intellect's power to "order" the configurations that make up the environment are largely subject to the limitations of man's senses and prior knowledge. Thus, the conceptualization of the Gorfs and Grimus has to start and end with the "real" in human terms.

So also with literary creation. A writer has to start with situations, characters, concepts, that readers can identify and relate to and *then* lead them into the unknown, the unfamiliar.

One of the obvious types of word-play used in the novel is the anagram.

The Gorfic obsession with anagram-making ranges from simple rearrangement of word-forms to the exalted level of the Divine Game of Order [. . .] the vast mental powers of the Gorfs make it possible for them anagrammatically to alter their very environment. *(Grimus 68/64-65)*

Anagrams provide the basic framework of the novel. Gorfs inhabit planet Thera, which orbits around the star Nus in the Yawy Klim galaxy of the Gorfic Nirveesu, and their leader is Dota. This is a string of simple anagrams: Toad is the leader of the race of Frogs that inhabit Earth, which moves around the Sun in the Milky Way galaxy of our Universe. The complexity lies in the identity of the Gorfs, which are very highly evolved frog-like creatures of rock. Just what is their function in the novel? They are like the Greek chorus, commenting on events but also participating in the action, transgressing the bounds of their roles.

The name "Grimus" is another important anagram. The demonic creator of Calf Island bears as its name an anagram of Simurg, "the Great Bird" which contains all other birds and in turn is contained by them (223/209). It is a mythical bird with esoteric associations in Arabic lore and Sufi writings. The choice of the bird as central symbol has its own expanding circles of connotations, as we shall see. At the anagrammatical level, it is significant that the author has chosen GRIMUS over other possible anagrams, several of which have their own thematic possibilities URGIMS, RUMGIS, SIRGUM – but GRIMUS is just right with its GRIM-US, GRIME-US, GRIMACE, GRIM-ACE, and associations of ANIMUS. It brings out the grim and grimy predicament of the life-force in a situation where the grimace replaces smiles and laughter. Thus, the anagram reaches deeper levels even as it works effectively at the superficial level.

Language is naming, it has been said. Thomas Carlyle says of names in *Sartor Resartus:* "what mystic influence does it not send inwards, even to the centre" and Michael Murphy, quoting him, adds, "The name surrounds us all our life like a cloak [. . . .] A name can shape a life."[4] Names grow inward and influence the bearer. But when an adult chooses a name for himself, he projects his own ideal image and strives thereafter to realize it, as happens with Grimus.

A word and its anagram contain the same components, but the anagram is also a distortion. Thus, by choosing an anagram of Simurg, Grimus proclaims that he would use Simurg's qualities but distort them to create something else. This could be the central metaphor of the novel: Creative power is; the diversity of life and values is due to what different people make of it, with it; all-pervading, all-embracing Simurg at one extreme and Grimus, a diabolical creator and controller, at the other.

Rushdie has obviously given considerable thought to his choice of names: There are numerous plainly functional puns such as the names of the Russian generals (Pissov, Sodov, Burgov and Phukov) and the specialists Kama(la) Sutra and Lee Kok Fook at the House of the Rising Son. The names of most major characters are functionally related to their dominant character-trait: Bird-Dog's dog-like devotion to the Great Bird; Axona (Axe owner); Eagle pitted against Simurg-Grimus; Liv Sylwan (Swanly); Livia Cramm (Live 'ere Cram) insatiable. Livia's husband's sensayuma (sense of humour), which leads him to pun on Jungfrau and Freudlein (25/25), and Nicholas Deggle's phrase of leave-taking – Ethiopia (Abyssinia = Ah'll be seein ya) = intimate awareness of the elaborate network of word-play that Rushdie has woven into the novel.

Anagrams are a rather simplistic device to advance the narrative and thematic thrust of the novel. Somewhat more complex is the device of using literary allusions to involve the reader in building his own parameters of comprehension and pleasure – what Fowler has called the reader's re-creative sympathy.

This re-creative sympathy is stimulated in two ways – first, by references to allusions outside the novel but within the reader's general knowledge, and then by allusions to the initial reference, so that there is an associative chain formed through the novel. To take an example: Gabriel Garcia Marquez, to whom Rushdie has often been likened in critiques of *Midnight's Children;* Kafka, who is never far from any serious work of contemporary fiction; T.S. Eliot and Lewis Carroll, who are favourites of Indo-English writers – all appear early in the novel and reappear intermittently. The town called K and the two spectres, Khallit and Mallit, conjured up by Gorf Koax bring to mind Kafka, and there are Kafkaesque nightmare-elements elsewhere; Khallit and Mallit tossing coins over seemingly meaningless banter recall Tom Stoppard's Rosencrantz and Guildenstern; the whirling Demons conjure up the fantasy of the

*Arabian Nights.* Later, several of these assume a part in one or other of the chain of events or symbols. K, for example, turns out to be the Arab letter Kaf, which has esoteric connotations and is also part of a rather atrocious pun, Bone of K = Kos (chaos). The reader's re-creative sympathy continues to associate Kafka's K and Kafkaesque frustration with Rushdie's K, even after he is told of Kaf and Kos.

Similarly, the isolation of Axona Plateau and Bird-Dog's visit to the plain, with its juke-boxes and automobiles, echo Garcia Marquez's *One Hundred Years of Solitude;* and even though Axona Plateau plays no part in the main story, the Garcia Marquez link continues to enrich the narrative for the reader who makes the initial connection.

There are innumerable phrases and quotations from various standard sources the collection of casual quotes that is part of an average person's literary baggage each serving a purpose in its context, but on deeper analysis found to be linked to a major theme in the novel; for example, the allusion to T.S Eliot's "Burnt Norton" in "'Go, go, go, said the bird'" (55/52) is termed a "digression" in the immediate context but can be linked by association to Eliot's "human kind/Cannot bear very much reality," which is one of the themes that Rushdie develops in *Grimus.*

One of the ways in which Rushdie uses allusions is through parallel citings; that is, by mentioning something or some act in the first part of the book and repeating something similar in the second part in such a way that it is not a direct link but is nevertheless related. As an example, the name Joe-Sue arises out of a literal ambiguity – "because my sex was uncertain until some time later" (15/16) – but it becomes a parallel for the subsuming of his identity with Grimus's in the last part; Dolores O'Toole resorting to Roman candles at the beginning seems gratuitous sensationalism until we find out about Flann O'Toole's impotence. The manner in which Dolores kills herself is identical to the way Liv kills herself. The Whirling Demons appear at the beginning, middle and end. While these references give structural balance to the story, the bird imagery and the Stone Rose are the central beams that hold up the narrative edifice.

The novel unfolds like a good detective story; the reader is given all the clues necessary to solve the mystery, but has to work at it. That the answers to all the puzzles posed in the novel are within the novel itself is the clue given in the first passage quoted above from the novel. The Chiefest Question is, *"And are we actually to be the least intelligent race in our Endimion?"* The answer is an anagram of the question; an elaborate reordering of the same fifty-six letters to read: *"Determine how catalytic an elite is; use our talent and learning-lobe" (69/65).* This sentence is rather heavy-handed, obviously Procrustean; however, it does indicate the method we should adopt for analysing the theme of the novel, and it also points out the elitist isolation that is intruded upon by Flapping Eagle.

The structure of the novel, which may be seen as an extended metaphor for Rushdie's technique, is very like Grimushome, which is described as a labyrinthine structure with a "bewildering series of interlocking rooms" (a description very appropriate, incidentally, to Rushdie's technique in *Midnight's Children).* One of the rooms is bare except for "two beautifully-detailed erotic sculptures"; one is full of birds, with a picture of Simurg, "the Roc of Sinbad, the Phoenix of myth"; one bears the carved letter "Kaf"; and one has shrouded outlines on podia; and there are bedrooms as well. Doors appear where there had been none. Thus we have various components of Rushdie's writing – interlocked pieces of erotica, symbols, mystery.

At the centre of this labyrinthine edifice is a small room which "went completely unnoticed" (257/241). This is the room of the Stone Rose; the power with which Calf Island had been created. There are literary elements of romances and fantasy in Grimus – the Rose as a Holy Grail, the wanderings of Flapping Eagle akin to the Ahaseurus myth. The Rose, in a romantic sense, is the symbol of the imagination. But since Jorge Luis Borges is one of Rushdie's favourite authors, it would be worthwhile looking for its sources in Borges.

Borges' stories "The Aleph" and "The Zahir" are of particular Significance. The connections are immediately apparent. Borges covers the A and the Z of the alphabet; *aleph,* the first letter of the Hebrew alphabet, is the equivalent of Greek *alpha* and Arabic *alit.* Borges is fond of using Arabic and Persian allusions; he also uses the letters because

> All language is an alphabet of symbols whose use presupposes a past *shared by all the other interlocutors. How,* then, transmit to others the infinite Aleph, which my fearful mind scarcely encompasses? [. . .] to signify the divinity, a Persian speaks of a bird that in some way *is* all birds.[5]

This could be the source of inspiration for Rushdie's "Kaf" and "Simurg." Other echoes of Borges are even more striking. Zahir, though literally a rose, is also "the shadow of the Rose and the rending of the Veil."[6] Rushdie uses the Dance of the Veils in the denouement; he combines the qualities of Aleph and Zahir in his rose: the Aleph gives a miraculous vision of the universe; and the Zahir eclipses everything. The Aleph is in the basement of a house, and the Rose is in a secret room; the narrator arranges various objects in the room as instructed and gets a vision. The Rose in *Grimus* is a set of stone slabs that can be arranged and aligned in different ways. Among the many things that the narrator sees in the Aleph are "all the ants in the world" and a "beach along the Caspian Sea"; Eagle, during his 700-year journey, sees "A *beach on which a maiden had been staked out naked, as giant ants moved up her thighs towards their goal" (32/32).*

The Rose, like the Aleph, is the object or abstraction through which one can control the Dimensions. In the novel, the controlling agent, the highest creative faculty, seems to be the Mind. Descartes' "I think, therefore I am," is changed by Dota and Grimus to "I think, therefore it is." Descartes' statement is never mentioned, but the narrative proceeds on the assumption that the reader's re-creative sympathy would make the connection through the author's play on words.

The main characters' superiority stems from their superior will-power and rational faculty, and not from any physical or imaginative strength. Virgil Jones, Eagle's mentor and guardian, is an obese, immobile fellow, like the Gorfs in intellect but like Oliver Hardy of the Laurel-and-Hardy team in appearance. His trousers, which have to be held up by his hands, make up a visual comic strip typical of Rushdie. Rushdie's excellence lies in the fact that he can give Virgil Jones the appearance of Oliver Hardy and Grimus himself that of the knitting sheep in Alice *Through the Looking Glass* and get away with it: that is, convince his readers of their superior powers.

I think, therefore it is. With a simple twist of a familiar phrase, Rushdie formulates the diabolical inspiration that brought Calf Island into existence.

Conceptualization is the greatest of creative powers. God said, Let there be Light, and there was Light. Nothing less than this will satisfy Grimus. Not taking a piece of clay and making a man or moulding a woman from his rib, not the creation of birds and beasts and the naming of them, no; it has to be the supreme creative power – of willing something out of nothing. Conceptualization.

Grimus, like Satan, tempts Eagle thrice. The first part of the Dance gives one the power to choose one's manner of death. The second is a Dance of Veils (associations of Salome and of the Hindu philosophy of Maya and of the Platonic idea of the world above and the reflection below) which reveals the "Ionic Structure of any Dynamic Essence" and thereby gives one control over that creature. The third is the power of Conceptualization. "Think of anywhere on the island. Anywhere at all," says Grimus. Eagle thinks of Dolores's hut, and the "cottage was here, in the room, in Grimushome" *(254/237)*.

This is the final marvel; after seeing it, Grimus is sure Eagle would willingly become his successor.

But Eagle resists all three temptations. Dolores's hysterical "Agape me" seems to work in Eagle's case. The tempter is driven backward. But here, with satanic cunning, Grimus wins. Through what might be called a Black Communion, Eagle and Grimus partake of each other through the Subsumer.

> *You swallow me. I swallow you.* [. . .] *You into me into you.* [. . .] *My son.* [. . .] You are my son, I give you my life *[259/242-43]*

"I was flapping Eagle. I was Grimus." Early in the novel, Rushdie alternates between the first-person and third-person point of view to show the contrapuntal movement of the protagonist's identity. The subsuming of Eagle-Grimus brings that chain to completion. While appearing to go off at random tangents in the course of the novel, Rushdie in reality has been a very careful architect in this work. "Who would write a story without knowing how it finished?," Grimus says of his plans for his own death, and thereby gives a clue to Rushdie's method, in which enormous effort has gone into the "effortless" balancing of weights.

There is a Death and there is a Resurrection, but on Grimus' terms, it seems. Eagle, having become part-Grimus, will be led by Grimus to continue Grimus's work, fostering Calf Island and reconceptualizing it at regular intervals, as Grimus had done. G'rimus, to all appearance, has won after the Subsuming. The Phoenix symbol, carefully built up all through the novel, is manifested in Grimus, as he is burnt to ashes. But Grimus has overlooked something. In the immolation of the mythical phoenix, the dross is destroyed and the gold reburnished. Rejuvenation has always been associated with purification. The purification takes place through Eagle's will-power. He wills himself to defeat the Grimus in him, no matter what the alternative to the Island is to be. It so happens that the alternative of this Mind-made, Mind-sustained creation is Nature. Flapping Eagle, who has never been good at solving puzzles the Gorf way, has instinctively made the right choice in keeping Media by his side and opposing Grimus, despite all the bribes offered by him. Perhaps Media grasping his hand in the final struggle between I-Eagle and I-Grimus turned the tide towards I-Eagle (269/251-52).1

Thus Nature, rather than Mind, wins in the end. Deprived of the conceptualizing power that had held it together, the island slowly disappears, "its molecules and atoms breaking dissolving, quietly vanishing into primal, unmade energy" (271/253).

The novel is based squarely in the English literary tradition, all save a handful of allusions taken from European classics, and it also includes science fiction and fantasy. The Gorfs remind one of *Star Wars* and more recent Steven Spielberg films, and it should be noted that Grimus predates all these; its occasional forays into sexual references foreslitadow the Laurence Sterne excesses of *Midnight's Children,* which incidentally borrows a lot from Sterne's digressive style.

As with many novelists, whereas Rushdie's second novel, *Midnight's Children, is* autobiographical, this, his first, is a carefully crafted literary exercise. Indeed, I could find only one inconsistency, a minor one, in the entire novel: after mentioning that "the 'voice' of the Gorf is only audible to the being it addresses" (97/91), Rushdie has Eagle listen to the debate between the Gorf and Mr Jones, "Flapping Eagle, eavesdropping, on half the eerie debate." But even this can be explained as the Gorf being meant to address Eagle.

Grimus has been ingeniously thought out, and, though difficult to unravel, is as precisely put together as a Rubik cube. It has literary characteristics that are more developed in *Midnight's Children:* the element of fantasy that commingles with the realistic; the concept of mind-travel; the enigmatic role of the Gorfs as a narrative framework akin to Padma's role in *Midnight's Children;* and a propensity to digress gratuitously into pornographic situations.

In this last context, one could always arrive at seemingly profound explanations for Flann O'Toole's chief pursuit in life and the extreme specializations of Madame Jocasta's girls at the House of the Rising Son; however, it seems to be more consistent with Rushdie's general style and vision that they are there for themselves, to add spice to life.

I would like to end on an Indian interpretation of one of the themes in Grimus: the theme of Creation and Dissolution. Rushdie refers only to the Greek version of the cyclical nature of creation. Grimus, when talking to Eagle about being his successor, says, "You are to be the next stage of the cycle, the next bearer of the flag, Hercules succeeding Atlas" (248/233). I would like to cite Hindu myths which are relevant to two main references in the novel – Dance and Dissolution – which come together in the final scene.

The Dance, as symbolic of creative power, is fundamental to many cultures. In Hinduism, the Dance is associated with the God Siva, one of whose names is Nataraja – King of Dance. This representation, expounded by such art historians as Ananda Coomaraswamy and by Balachandra Rajan in his *The Dark Dancer,* is one of the most familiar of Hindu sculptures: Nataraja with waving locks and raised left foot, circled with a ring of flames and with his right foot on a demon-dwarf usually identified as Ignorance. Siva's dance is the dance of Creation and of Dissolution. In the beginning, to the sound of his drum (the Big Bang theory of modern astronomy), the universe came into being. During each cycle of existence, he, as Nataraja, sustains the universe by maintaining the equilibrium of forces – of nature, for example. Then, in a crescendo of movement, he dissolves the universe back into formless energy. Another cycle begins. Each *mahayuga,* as the cycle is called, lasts about four and a half million years, and there have been countless *mahayugas.*

Calf Island is a microcosm of the last period of a cycle. In Hindu mythology, during the last quarter of each cycle the world is taken over by a demonic force, and the cycle ends with the destruction of that force and the dissolution of existence as known theretofore. The battle between the Prince of Darkness and the Prince of Light in Zoroastrian mythology could have been Rushdie's actual source. Or it could have been the Greek cycle of Kronos-Saturn-Zeus or any of its equivalents in other mythologies. However, the Hindu equivalent certainly comes to mind as one reads *Grimus,* because the concept of formless energy taking form and then dissolving into formlessness is so integral to Hindu speculations about creation and time, as is the concept of evil forces temporarily usurping the suzerainty of the forces of good.

Grimus is a first novel. Rushdie's subsequent novels, *Midnight's Children* and *Shame,* seem to indicate that he has found his voice against the setting of his native land (now the two countries of India and Pakistan). But I would predict that, once Rushdie gets a series of short stories (present germinally in his recent novels), he will return to the literary tradition that forms the basis of Grimus, and enrich that tradition as he has enriched the post-colonial literature of the erstwhile British Raj.

## Notes

1. Roger Fowler, *Linguistics and the Navel,* London: Methuen (1977), 3.

2. Salman Rushdie, Grimus,(London: Granada/Panfier, 1981, and Grafton 1985 [1975): 69/65. Subsequent parallel references to these editions are in the text, the 1981 edition first and 1975 second.
3. Gunther Anders, *Ka/ka – Pro and Contra,* tr. A. Steer & A.K. Thorlby (London: Bodley Head, *1960* [German *1946/1953]): passim.*
4. Michael Murphy, *Golf in the Kingdom.* New York: Dell (1972): 11.
5. Jorge Luis Borges, "The Aleph," tr. Anthony Kerrigan, in *A Personal Anthology,* ed. & intro. Anthony Kerrigan (London: Jonathan Cape, 1968): 149.
6. "The Zahir," tr. Anthony Kerrigan, in *A Personal Anthology, 136.*

## Works Cited

Anders, Gunther. *Kafka – Pro and Contra,* tr. A. Steer & A.K. Thorlby. London: Bodley Head, 1960 (German 1946/1953).

Borges, Jorge Luis. *A Personal Anthology,* ed. & intro. Anthony Kerrigan. London: Jonathan Cape, 1968.

Fowler, Roger. *Linguistics and the Novel.* New Accents series. London: Methuen, 1977. Murphy, Michael. *Golf in the Kingdom.* New York: Dell, 1972.

Rushdie, Salman. *Grimus.* London: Granada/Panther, 1981 and Grafton 1985 (1975).

# 8

# An Analysis of *Shame*

As one reads each new novel by an author, one comes across repetitions of phrases or events or characters from earlier novels, which give a momentary pleasure of recognition. For a critic, repetitions take on more weight for they might be related to the author's narrative methodology or vision of life.

Repetition is one of Rushdie's distinctive narrative devices. "*The Leitmotif*," he has said, is a kind of non-conventional symbolism where

> you use as recurring things in the plot incidents or objects or phrases which in themselves have no meaning or no particular meaning but which form a kind of non-rational network of connections in the book. (*Kunapipi* VII: 1, 3)

In this interview, Rushdie goes on to explain how he used the leitmotif idea to "orchestrate what is otherwise a huge mass of material." A leitmotif provides a backbone to the narrative. And if a repetition spans several different works, it reveals something about the author's vision of life or at least about his

---

This was Chapter VII of *The Perforated Sheet*, 1988.

preferences. It is worthwhile listing ideas and references that recur in Rushdie's fiction.

*Peripheral Hero*: All three novels have a " peripheral hero" as Rushdie calls Omar Khayyam Shakil in *Shame.* Shakil is called a peripheral hero and feels himself to be one. Saleem Sinai *thinks* he is at the centre of events even though he occasionally recognizes that he is at the periphery of action, that he is one to whom things are done, not one by whom things are done. In a talk at a conference in Goteborg in 1982, Rushdie said Saleem is the essential child in every adult, a child that thinks the world revolves around itself. But Rushdie and the reader know he is not a centre-stage hero. Flapping Eagle in *Grimus* is peripheral in the same way Saleem is in that he is acted upon most of the time and rarely initiates action, but he is more essentially bound to Grimus than Saleem is to India or Shakil to Pakistan or to Sufiya, and thereby he becomes the central figure by the end of the novel.

*Home as a Character:* In all three novels, a house associated with the protagonist shares certain common characteristics and exerts similar influence. Grimushome, Methwold-Estate and Nishapur are all sprawling mansions with endless spaces in which the protagonist gets lost. Each has a life of its own, as it were, and exerts a potent force-field, malevolent and intimidating as in *Grimus* and *Shame,* protective but stifling in *Midnight's Children.* They are old, and cluttered with an accumulated wealth of artifacts and memories that hold their inmates in thrall. The ghosts of the past seem to be their real masters while the living tenant is fugitive. They shield inmates from the outside world and therefore are havens of security, as for Nadir Khan in *Midnight's Children.* But they are also prisons which shackle their inmates who long to escape as young Shakil does in *Shame;* Rani Humayhn is imprisoned in the Harappa house at Mohenjo. Methwold's whimsical condition, in *Midnight's Children,* that nothing should be changed within the house exercises a hold on the Sinais even when they are freed of this obligation. This short-term imposition of stasis by Methwold is linked to the long-term freezing of Ahmed Sinai's assets, both financial and sexual.

Rushdie's art endows each house with its own idiosyncrasies of appearance, action and influence.

In *Shame,* Bariamma's house is a "forest of new relatives," "a blood jungle" where Bilquis has to share a "cavernous bedroom" with forty other female relatives. Rushdie's description of the husbands' stealthy entry and lovemaking seems unadulterated fantasy but it is only an exaggeration, not fabrication. Attia Hosain's sensitive and realistic novel, *Sunlight on a Broken Column,* also refers to such a dormitory set-up on a terrace. Exaggeration but not fantasy. The same is true of the Harappa house. In the "backyard of the universe" in Sind, the Harappa mansion is a huge structure, furnished with the opulence of decades – paintings framed in gilt, Sheraton chairs cut-glass decanters arid thick carpets.

In all three novels, the main house is destroyed, razed to the ground. Methwold's palaces are replaced by "a great pink monster of a building" (*MNC,* 452), the natural result of the city's growth and industrialization; but the other two are destroyed in unnatural ways: Grimushome, along with the entire world of Calf island, unmade itself, "its molecules and atoms breaking, dissolving, quietly vanishing into primal, unmade energy."(*G,* 270). Nishapur is destroyed loudly in an explosion. All three vanish completely. You can't go home again.

*Power over people:* All three novels have characters who have some quality that makes them different from others around them, a faculty that given them power over people. Grimus' power over Calf Island is total. Each Midnight's Child has a different kind of power. *In Shame,* certain characters who make a momentary appearance in *Midnight's Children* are developed into full-blown, figures the boy who "had completely mastered, by the age of ten, the lost arts of alchemy, with which he regenerated the fortunes of his ancient but dissipated house" (*MNC,* 199) becomes Shakil, the peripheral hero of *Shame.* The Baudi twins "who possessed the ability of making every man who saw them fall hopelessly . . . in love with them," becomes Arjumand Harappa who has the added power of evoking similar passion in members of her own sex as well. Sundari, the girl who was so beautiful that she blinded all who saw her and later is disfigured, is transformed into Sufiya Zinobia whose blushes generate such intense heat that it makes her bathwater scalding hot and burns

Bariamma's lips when, she kisses her cheek. Saleem's clairvoyance is transferred to Talvar Ulhaq.

However, in *Shame* there is a rational basis to these magical qualities. They are Rushdie's narrative devices to convey his message about shame and shamelessness and his satire of Pakistan's politics and social values. Talvar's clairvoyance which "helped him in his police work to divine where crimes were going to be committed before the thieves had worked it out themselves, so that his record of arrests was unbeatable (*S*,164).

is Rushdie's method of satirizing the police just as the Magicians' power to disappear and reappear in *Midnight's Children* is his comment on police evacuation of Delhi slums and to quick reappearance of the slum-dwellers in a new or old slums at some other place.

Talvar's choice of Naveed "on account of the hunger of your womb"(*S*,163) does not imply clairvoyance so much as his practical common sense and a certain amount of natural chemistry. Then Rushdie goes on to make Talvar and Naveed symbolic of Pakistan; Talvar Ulhaq (Sword of the Faith) and Good News set out to breed the post-partition generation. Their procreative prowess is another way of stating that there was a runaway growth in population. Naveed is the land and Talwar the martial hand; they get married on the day Yahya Khan ousted Ayub Khan and took over the, government. Naveed "proved utterly incapable of coping with the endless stream of humanity flowing out between her thighs" (*S*, 207) and "the Administrator's home had began to resemble an orphanage more than a seat of government" (*S*, 226). Naveed's suicide is a prophetic statement of what is likely to come. Naveed's name ("Good News") is carefully chosen to fit into the symbolic framework. Of all: the characters endowed with superhuman powers, Flapping Eagle is the only one who "survives," who uses his powers to achieve a certain measure of success, a certain victory.

*Names and Word-play:* Rushdie's choice of names is not random. Word-play in Grimus is so consistent and integral to the plot that it is studied elsewhere in this volume. Rushdie's play on names occurs in all three novels. As with the four Russian generals in Grimus – Pissov, Sodov, Bugrov and Phukov there are three generals in *Shame.* Raddi (filth) Bekar (Useless) and

Phisaddi (laggard). Rushdie's comment on army rule is implicit in his choice of names. The significance of the names Omar Khayyam and Nishapur is clear in their contrast to the originals. The choice of Shakil is typical of Rushdie's word play. Shakil is phonetically similar to *shakal* which in Hindi-Urdu means 'face'. Further, Shakil and Hyder are slight phonetic deviations from Jekyll and Hyde, the-beauty-and-the-beast sides of Zinobia Shakil nee Hyder. Sufiya (Sufi being a religious sect) and Zinobia (Xenophobia, fear of strangers) are, again, carefully chosen names. Mohenjo Daro and Harappa, centres of ancient civilizations, are not functional nomenclatures but they have reverberations, the magic of the past, and charisma is consistent with Harappa's playboy personality.

**Minor Recurring Motifs**

There are numerous minor instances of repetitions and echoes in the novels. All three use the fantastic mode but *Grimus* carries it farthest. The idea of evolving people and places which transcended the physical limitations of everyday human life clearly interests Rushdie. So much so that he repeats in *Shame* the kind of speculation on which all of Grimus is based. Rushdie's voice interrupts the narrative at the point when Bariamma agrees to let Bilquis and Raza leave her home to set up on their own to muse on the myths of anti-gravity or the anti-myths of gravity as he calls it. If a pharmaceutical company or NASA were to come up with an anti gravity pill, he speculates, there would be personalized international travel etc. etc. (*S*, 86). All his protagonists defy the laws of nature.

*Grimus* and *Shame* are circular-narratives, beginning and ending at the same place. In *Shame,* the circularity is forced, but more of that later.

*Shame* and *Midnight's Children* have many common elements including historical events and characters. The initial allegory in both are linked to the British-India connection. Omar's three mothers could well be India, West Pakistan, and East Pakistan (now Bangladesh); his father is English. Saleem brings together in himself English, Hindu and Muslim components of India. Methwold's insistence that nothing be changed in the house directly spills over into his allegory, "a very Indian lust for allegory" as he says (*S*, 96). He has decided to leave everything behind, in suitable hands. He certainly has the last laugh, as it turns out, with his bastard child being left "absolutely intact" in the Sinais' able hands: Omar's English fattier is never identified and what might be the allegory there? The three mothers imposed their will, their machinations on the *Angrez*, as perhaps Jinnah did?

Mary Pereira and Hasmat Bibi, the two nurses, are kindred spirits, jealously guarding secrets and fiercely 'loyal.

The movie, *Gaiwallah*, occurs in both novels as does teenage adoration of a playback singer. When young, both Omar and, Saleem are overly preoccupied with their sexual appetite or curiosity rather, and both become voyeurs.

*Voyeurism*: This recurring theme may be linked to Rushdie's vision of art. Shakil, as a boy growing up in Nishapur, uses his hypnotic power to be a voyeur, of the male servants' homosexual acts and heterosexual fantasies; Saleem, likewise, visits every brothel in town through his clairvoyance. Sexual voyeurism is part of adolescence, Rushdie seems to say. And some people never grow up, obviously. Rushdie's favourite psychological representation is invested in a mystic moment: Omar Khayyam Shakil crosses the boundary at the exact moment that he first sees Farah Zoroaster through his grandfather's telescope

> he felt his voice break in his throat while below his belt other things slid downwards too, to take their appointed places, somewhat ahead of schedule, in hitherto empty sacs. (*S*, 35)

Saleem also reaches puberty prematurely, and Rushdie has him state it very bluntly in a parenthetical statement (*MNC*, 241).

All the metaphors and descriptions for voyeurism – the conducted tour of the House of the Rising Son and Jocasta's watch over her proteges; the perforated sheet, Lifafa's peepshow and Saleem's clarivoyant wanderings; the fragments of broken mirrors, Shakil's telescope and, his night circuits – on his own and with Isky – represent both message and method in Rushdie. A writer, and the reader too for that matter, is a voyeur, who sees what he normally should not see and who can never see anything in its entirety.

*The Concept of Qaf*: But the desire to see everything, know about everything, experience everything, is as inherent in human beings as their inability to do so. Desire, idealistically, presupposes or implies the possibility of fulfilment. And the secret formula for fulfilment is enshrined in Kaf. This is another of Rushdie's favourite concepts. Whereas in *Grimus,* Calf Island is of major significance and Kaf mountain and Simurg the mythic bird are integral to the novel, the reference to Kaf in *Shame is* there only because the concept fascinates Rushdie. Within its immediate context, the reference is appropriate enough. One day, when Shakil is ten and a half years old, a walnut screen is removed from his grandfather's study to be sent to the pawnbroker and Shakil sees that on it, was portrayed the mythical, circular mountain of Qaf complete with the thirty birds playing God thereupon and behind the screen was

> a bookcase stuffed with volumes on the theory acid practice of hypnosis; Sanskrit mantras, compendiums of the lore of the Persian Magi . ., an account of the hypno-exorcisms of Father Gassner, (*S*, 33)

Qaf, like Ganges on the Hindu imagination, wields a powerful influence on Rushdie and becomes a symbol. His fascination with this concept is his undoing in *Shame. Shame is a* fractured novel in several ways. The split between Shakil's story and Isky-Raza's is the most obvious one. Shakil's is in the fabulous or 'fantastic' mode, Isky-Raza's in the satirical. Whereas *Midnight's Children* combines the two satisfactorily, *Shame* does not. Several factors contribute to this.

*Shame as a fractured narrative*: The very massiveness of the earlier novel precludes reader-expectation of a tightly-structured narrative; the reader readily accepts what Saleem says in the opening paragraphs there are so many stories to tell, too many, such an excess of intertwined lives events miracles places rumours, so dense a commingling of the improbable and the mundane.

But *Shame* does not encompass the vast panorama *Midnight's Children* does. It deals only with a handful of individuals – the Hyders, the Harappas, and Shakil. The earlier novel successfully communicates a feeling of the multitudes and.

colour against which the central action takes place, whereas in *Shame* the background is as faceless as the desert of Sind or barren mountaintops of Quetta. The similes, to a certain extent, contain both the message and the method: that Pakistan is a desert, and by blurring the background Rushdie is expressing the facelessness of the population in the political context.

In an interview published in Kunapipi (VII:1, 1985), Rushdie has. said that "the family is so central to life in India" that he took that as the axis for *Midnight's Children* and that he used the family context in *Shame* as well; though "in real life the families of Zia and Bhutto are not connected," he related them because:

> What I wanted to say is that in this society . . . . there is a kind of Gogolian system where the ruling clan is minute and politics is a kind of family quarrel.

Rushdie's point about the centrality of family in politics and in culture is well-taken. In India, the Nehru dynasty has established that most marvellous modern innovation: monarchy-in-a-democracy. If Benazir Bhutto could have her way, he says, so would it be in Pakistan.

However convincing this interpretation and rationale is in the light of allegory, no novel can be justified on account of its partial allegorical content alone. Rushdie would be the first to accept this, as he has said in the interview cited above. The narrative structure has to stand on its own, and in *Shame* it does not. There is no substantive link between the boy who devoured and digested the secrets of Qaf in the shadow of Q's upside down mountains and Shakil, the debauched doctor. True, both are obese (like Virgil Jones), both are voyeurs indulging in sexual orgies, but the resemblance stops there. The vision of the mountains of the holy land are given over to mad Maulana Dawood (ironic that Rushdie should choose the name of the author whose translation of the Koran he has used) to fan his fanaticism; Shakil uses his hypnotic powers once, and by inference more often, on Zinobia to get the beast in her under control; but that is all we hear of the knowledge he had ingested from the books presided over by the mythical circular mountain of Qaf, complete with the thirty birds playing God thereupon. Shakil could have played God and used the hypno-exorcisms of

Father Gassner but he does not play even the devil with any conviction. As to Rushdie's intent about "the peripheral man" that "writing the history of such a man would seem to me to be writing the history of many other people," (Kunapipi, VII, 1, 1985), Shakil does not come through as such. He is an individual, a freak, and thank God for that. Even on Pakistan, "a miracle gorse wrong," "a failure of the dreaming mind" we would not wish such a curse!

This failure of potential seems typical of Rushdie's characters. It is not a natural Wordsworthian loss of "the youth who daily farther from the east must travel" but a conscious, wanton betrayal. Isky and Raza had even less to do with Shakil's betrayal of his initial potential than the widow had to do with the *Midnight's Children* of theirs; and even in the latter case, as has been analyzed elsewhere in this volume, the talented's betrayal of themselves and their country was far more inexcusable than the Widow's betrayal of them.

However, the fracture in *Shame* is not one of the message alone but of method as well. Shakil's characterization is only one of the factors. The flaw is architecturally in the foundation pillars themselves. Shakil's story moves off base. "If you hold down one thing, you hold down the adjoining," the narrator says (*S*, 173). The corollary is that if one thing gives way, so does the adjoining, and as he goes on to say, "In the end, though, it all blows up in your face." This metaphor for dictatorships is equally appropriate for the structure of a novel.

To continue with the architectural analogy, the two main foundation posts are Shakil's story and Isky-Raza's story. They are connected by a central beam: Shakil is Isky's partner in debauchery and later becomes Raza's son-in-law. Shakil born at Nishapur, seeks asylum there for Ran and both are killed in acts of vengeance, Raza by the three mothers for having caused their younger son's death and Shakil by Zinobla for not doing what husbands are supposed to do. A very balanced edifice, one should conclude. Two pillars connected by a crossbeam to hold up all the rest, and the whole within a circular frame where beginning and end neatly join. Neat, too neat, and therein lies the problem. As Elfrida says in *Grimus*,

> It's too pretty, too neat. I do not care for stories that are so, so tight. Stories should be like life, slightly frayed at the edges, full of loose ends,, lives juxtaposed by accident rather than some grand design. (*G*, 149-150)

Now let us clear up an apparent inconsistency, for criticism, alas or fortunately, has to be consistent. A tight structure is not in itself wrong for a story; nor is there any intrinsic merit in loose ends. The point is that each story needs a certain type of form. Isky-Harappa's story needs a tight structure. Unlike the earlier novel, *Shame is* very definitely and mainly a political novel (cf. *Kunapipi, 1985)* and the medium of the satire is a joint family, in keeping with the size and politics of Pakistan. Whereas *Midnight's Children* is about all of India, *Shame is* only about the politics of Pakistan. Names and events are thinly veiled, unlike the heavy burqa of its women. It is the story of Isky (Bhutto) and Raza (Zia), two presidents of Pakistan; the story of how Bhutto seeking to perpetuate his power by keeping the army in his pocket appointed "the most incompetent general" as commander-in-chief so that he need not fear insubordination or an army take-over. But "the idea that a general is likely to remain in your pocket is a very stupid and dangerous idea." (Kunapipi, 1985). Zia ousted Bhutto, had him hanged, and set up a regime of religious bigotry. In the larger context, the novel shows the corruption and violence of all dictatorships – Bhutto's and Zia's and their predecessors'. Within its immediate context, the Isky-Raza story presents no problems. The admixture of exaggeration and essential historical realism is effective. Whether or not the characterization of the friends-turned-rivals is true to their originals', the message that a country can be, and has been, run by such men is not only credible but very insightful. It conveys something essential about the political history of Pakistan.

Within the Isky-Raza story, Rushdie packs an arsenal of satire: indiscriminate and. groundless police arrests (by Talvar as mentioned above); the farce of elections where re-counts set right those results which prior coercion had failed to bring in line (*S*. 178); Raza's Gichki-Needle Valley ruthlessness *(S,* 102-104); Haroun Harappa's rich-boy tantrums *(S*. 147-150); bribery as a part of Customs officers' life styles (*S*, 51); Isky's "diplomatic" persecution of Soviet and American ambassadors (S. 185) being some of the notable episodes.

Rushdie also uses authorial intrusions to comment on specific social and political ills: the long joke about Zia's deal with God (*S,* 112); a comment on Islamic fundamentalism being imposed from government: levels (*S,* 251); an interlude on various aspects of everyday life tit Pakistan (*S,* 68-69); an anecdote to illustrate how informers infiltrate social get-togethers and how cleverly they are fooled (*S,* 27); all these are authorial digressions that are tacked on to the Isky-Raza story but are functional and therefore achieve a harmony within the narrative structure.

But the Shakil-Zinobia story belongs to another Dimension, to take an analogy from Grimus. No wonder the whirling Demons do not allow the two to co-exist harmoniously.

In itself, this story, though split in another way, is powerful. It successfully fuses elements of fairy-tale with a profound insight into that strange, emotional configuration, Sharam or Shame.

The fairy-tale is, predictably, inverted. A Rushdie inversion is fairly straight-forward; it uses familiar correlatives and turns them around, as with a prince turning into a frog or a princess, devouring the dragon Instead of a beautiful princess in a tower, we have an ugly, fat boy; instead of a tyrannical ogre, we have three too-loving mothers; instead of a wizard who can change into different forms, we have three who coalesce into one. And people do get married but they never ever live happily after.

The idea of the three mothers is probably original. Though Kartikeya, son of the God Siva, was nursed by six mothers, the literary forebears of the Shakil sisters are more likely *Macbeth's* witches and Donald Duck's three nephews who complete each other's sentences. Their characterization is brilliant. They grow into one through their common resentment of their father and their desire and decision to have a baby. They "began to resemble each other so closely that even the servants made mistakes" (*S,* 19). But with Omar's fateful demand on his twelfth birthday "to, let me out of this horrible house," the three-in-one identity breaks. Though they retain their unanimity by an effort of will long enough to decide on Omar's immediate future, their common identity fractures and Rushdie introduces yet another ingenious coalescing by having the wrong heads ending upon the wrong bodies. "They became psychological centaurs, fish-women, hybrids" (*S*, 40).

In order to bring the story full circle, Rushdie has them having yet another son, Babar, who gets killed in Raza's skirmish at Needle Valley so that they can kill him at the end of the novel. Somewhat contrived but let it pass for the present.

In the Shakil-Zinobia story, Zinobia is Rushdie's main subject and message. He rather peremptorily drops the. "Nishapur thread of narrative to start Part II of the novel with the words, "This is a novel about Sufiya Zinobia . . . .or. . .Sufiya Zinobia is about this novel."

Sufiya Zinobia is an embodiment of Shame, and Shakil the embodiment of shamelessness. Shame and shamelessness are the "roots to violence" (*S*, 116). The concept of Sharam, as Rushdie says (*S*, 30), is difficult to translate. It is a configuration of emotions, "embarrassment, discomfiture, decency, modesty, shyness, the sense of having an ordained place in the world." Zinobia is the fusion of three figures as Rushdie explains (*S*, 115-118). One is a Pakistani girl in the East End of London whose father killed her for having made love to a white boy. Her act had brought dishonour on his family, and only her blood could wash away the stain. Her father and his fellow Asians saw his act as a ritual of atonement, not of Retribution on the girl or of murder. Gaza's staking himself to the post at Harappa's Mohenjo is a single ritualistic act. To the list Rushdie has given above should be added perhaps the word "honour."

The second figure who has gone into the making of Zinobia is a boy from a news clipping, who was found blazing in a parking lot, in what seemed to be an auto-ignited fire without the aid of any external fuel or flame. Like him or like one of *Midnight's Children*, Zinobia's blushes are of preternatural origin and intensity.

The third figure is an imaginary one conjured up by Rushdie's musings on subway assaults on girls who out of shame do not report or talk about the incident and on street violence that comes from humiliated, frustrated youngsters: He imagines the assaulted girl throwing herself on her attackers "breaking arms legs noses balls, without knowing whence the violence came, without seeing how she, so slight a figure, could command such awesome strength" (*S*, 117).

"Humiliate people for long enough and a wildness bursts out of them," he says. That's how it is with Zinobia. Humiliated because she is not the sex her parents desired her to be, she becomes sensitive from birth to this emotion of shame. She "blushed for the world, absorbing like a sponge ball the emotions that should have been felt, but were not – such as regret for a harsh word, guilt for a crime, embarrassment, propriety, shame" (*S*, 122). She was a saint. "A saint is a person who surfers in our stead." But she is also a beast generated and fed by constant humiliation not just her own but the world's.

In line with the fantastic element, Rushdie exaggerates around a realistic core when developing Zinobia's characteristics. Mentally retarded children are known to be stronger of hold than their normal counterparts. They will not easily let go of what they have in hand and reach for whatever they want with a single-mindedness of purpose that seems to give them unnatural strength. They are usually unaware of their obstinacy and physical power.

Rushdie's characterization is superb, full of pathos for the beauty in her, so that even after her gruesome decapitation of Pinkie Aurangzeb's 218 turkeys, even after her attack on Talvar where she almost made him the two hundred and nineteenth headless creature, the reader can still sympathize compassionately with her as she takes her favourite toys and games out of her head and plays with them. The long passage is handled with the care that its fragility demands; and it shows a sensitiveness and gentleness that is rare, very rare, in Rushdie:

> when people are present she never dares to take the things out and play with them in case they get taken away or broken by mistake . . . . One of the best inside-things is when her father picks her up . . . . She takes him out of her head and makes him do it all over again . . . . You can't do that with the things outside your head. Sometimes they happen only once and you have to be quick and grab them and stuff

> them' away in your secret place. Sometimes they never happen at all. (*S*, 213)

But she makes them happen and puts them in so she can take them out and play. Like her favourite game: skipping rope with her mother. With unparalleled tenderness, Rushdie shows her yearning for parental love, her love for babies, her troubling, vague memories of her past acts of violence, her six-year-old mind in her nineteen-year-old body grappling uncomprehendingly with the secret kept from her of what husbands do that her husband did with her nurse. It is this last frustrating secret that awakens the Beast in her once again.

She knows that Shahbanou does it for her. (The Shahbanou Shakil team is an exact replication of Dolores O'Toole-Virgil Jones partnership, she scrawny and stubborn, he fat and superior.) When, ten years later, Shahbanou gets pregnant, and leaves, Zinobia decides she wants it for herself, and goes out to get it. "Four husbands come and go. . .and then her hands reach for the first boy's neck. The others stand still and wait their turn" (*S*, 219). With her hypnotic eyes she holds them, and then one by one, twists their heads off.

At this time, Zinobia at 28 had a mental age of nine and a half. Just why Shakil, that very knowledgeable doctor, did not know his patient's need to be a wife is a question one would ask in the Isky-Raza story. But in the Shakil-Zinobia story one is not troubled by this digression from realism. One is quite willing to accept a suspension of disbelief and even go along with Zinobia's ghastly violence in itself and as expression of Rushdie's larger message regarding humiliation. The fusion of magic realism and satire is credible and harmonious. If this kind of violence were to erupt in Pakistan, we would "understand" it the same way fellow Asians and I and even Rushdie himself "understood" the Pakistani father in London, who killed his daughter.

This story calls for loose ends, for frayed edges. But Rushdie forces the Isky-Raza story into this and draws the iron hoop of circularity around them. Zinobia need not have been Raza's daughter to have come into Shakil's life. For the attraction she held for him is squarely within his Nishapur phase. It had its origins in his hero worship of Edouardo Roderigues, who, in an act of self sacrifice, married Farah Zoroaster who was in age and relationship like a daughter to him. Imitating him, Shakil is attracted by the self-sacrificing situation of marrying an idiot-girl thirty years younger to himself.

By making Zinobia the daughter of Raza, and Shakil the bosom friend of Isky; Rushdie forces certain movements; he brings Shakil from the periphery to the vortex of action and thereby makes him answerable to questions that arise in the moral and political context. Moreover, he pulls Shakil from the plane of magic realism to the plane of political satire; and finally, he makes Zinobia an instrument of retribution instead of an instrument of irrational violence. The three mothers torturing him for having been a time server and thus betraying the hopes they'd had when christening him Omar Khayyam of Nishapur, is all the circularity and retribution that the ending needed.

*Shame as History*: There is a difference between history and the historical. "Historical" implies a compendium of data, of dates, names, battles, coups: and other details pertaining to events. " History" implies an interpretation of the historical in order to bring about an understanding of the past and its relation to the present.

*Shame is* a history but it is only skeletally historical. *Shame* deals with a small canvass and the main characters are thinly veiled representations of real people; indeed, Salman's veils are so much thinner than Salome's legendary veils, and the acts of corruption ascribed to presidents and generals of Pakistan are so specific that one needs to declare loudly a note of caution. The main figures and movements in the Isky-Harappa story are historically true but most of the specific details are not. However, Rushdie's interpretation of historical events is very perceptive.

Rushdie makes several significant comments about the recent history of Pakistan. The metaphor that expresses his summation most aptly is in the episode of Bilquis' fire ordeal. – In the summer of 1947, her father's movie theatre, appropriately named Empire Talkies, is burnt to the ground as Delhi entered the dawn-of independence from the British Empire. Her clothes were blown off and she stood infant-naked except for her muslin dupatta. Rescued and wooed by Captain Raza Hyder, she flies with him to Pakistan, that "new, moth-nibbled land of God."(*S*, 67). Bilquis' nakedness is representational of Pakistan.

Partition stripped Pakistan of its past in two ways: Muslims who were in India fled to the newly-created country leaving their pasts behind; Muslims in Pakistan, he goes on to say, were totally disoriented.

> The city's old inhabitants; who had become accustomed to living in a land older than time . . . . had been given a bad shock by independence, by being told to think of themselves, as well as the country itself, as new.

In other words, even those who had stayed where they had always been were disoriented by the new ideology of the times.

To build Pakistan it was necessary to cover up Indian history, to deny that Indian centuries lay just beneath the surface of Pakistani Standard Time. The past was rewritten. (*S*, 87)

The irony; Rushdie says, was that the new history was written by mohajirs, the immigrants who had come from India and who now went into their new life with passion – be it hate or ambition. The original inhabitants were totally passed over:

> it was the ones who, really were new, the distant; cousins and half acquaintances and total strangers who poured in from the – east to settle in the Land of God, who took over and got things going. (*S*, 81)

Corruption ran rampant. The new historians' history lacked something and the palimpsest they drew on the old kept peeling away. Rushdie's idea about layers of history is intriguing. He sees the failure of Pakistan as being due to the friction between the old and the new, "the obscured world forcing its way back through what-had-been-imposed" (*S*, 87). But the original inhabitants of the country, he has said, were overridden by the new. In spite of their passivity, their very presence, the accumulated inertia of centuries perhaps, deters the palimpsest from gluing itself firmly. Or, it could be that the new historians work fast, not giving it enough time to dry *into* the old layer.

When comparing *Shame* with other partition-novels, one notes that there are no communal massacres reported and there is no Hindu-Muslim conflict. The reason lies in the historical fact that almost all the Hindus of the region were either massacred or driven out. Modern historians might be able to advise modern politicians on how this might have bearing on the more contemporary communal conflict in the Punjab.

Another point of interest about Rushdie's comment on history is what he says of secession:

> When individuals come unstuck from their native land, they are called migrants. When nations do the same thing (Bangladesh), the act is called secession. (*S*, 86)

Pakistan seceded from India and hence the "emptiness of one's luggage". "We have come unstuck from more than land. We have floated upwards from history, from memory, from Time" (*S*, 87).

Given Bangladesh's double secession, it would seem an irresistible subject for Rushdie's next novel, even though he has said *Shame* is likely to be the last he will write on his native land which has tripled since his birth.

Pakistan is a "a failure of the dreaming mind" is what *Shame* says. Without history, without any worthwhile goal or incentive, the suppressed violence of shame has only erupted into violent self-destruction. *Midnight's Children,* despite the failure of dream and the preponderance of political oppression is somehow far more optimistic about the future of India than *Shame* is of the future of Pakistan. Saleem's son is not his, and his son's son may not be his son's but there is a sense of continuity despite adversity even in the last terribly depressing paragraph *of Midnight's Children.* But nothing in *Shame* and certainly not the ending, leaves anything hopeful.

If *Shame* is indeed Rushdie's last novel on the Indian subcontinent, it is a sad note on which to part ways.

## Works Cited

Salman Rushdie. *Shame* (London: Picador, 1983). Subsequent quotations are from this edition.

# 9

# Salman Rushdie's *Shame*

## An Overview of a Labyrinth

Salman Rushdie's *Midnight's Children (1981)* and *Shame (1983)* are a critic's delight. Like young Omar Khayyam Shakil wandering through his home of countless rooms, each rich with the dust and secrets of decades; like Dr. Aadam Aziz seeing his future wife in parts through a perforated sheet; like Flapping Eagle questing through Dimensions for Grimus, we can spend timeless hours walking through the labyrinthine corridors of Rushdie's novels.

But faced with the task of encompassing several cogent lines of analysis within a prescribed framework of time and space, one is right away afflicted with temporary paralysis. One of the ways out of this predicament is to take an aerial view of the labyrinth before entering it, to study game plans, and decide on one's areas of play. Certain patterns emerge as one studies an aerial view of the labyrinth:

1. Because of the unfamiliarity of the terrain, students, especially those outside the Indian subcontinent, would

---

This essay was published in *The New Indian Novel in English: A Study of the 1980s*. Ed. Viney Kirpal. Bombay: Allied Publishers. 1990. pp. 121-130.

appreciate a rather detailed explication of certain political and cultural landmarks.

2. The maps that are provided by critics and by Rushdie in his interviews are not always reliable.
3. The novel is not a fantasy or fabulation but has a realistic core. One of the major techniques used is of stretching a reference to its utmost limit and then some. Two analogies that may express this are of a singer stretching a note on a breath that seems endless and of a glassblower shaping a stem of glass into elaborate coils and forms in one continuous movement.
4. The maze is ingenious but there is a certain element of trickery in that there are two separate circuits, each with its own entrance and exit; the two circuits are connected at different points so that an unwary player might think they are the same and struggle to figure out his coordinates using wrong data. Solving a Rubik's Cube that has two faces of the same colour might actually he easier, but not if you are unaware of this, quirk and have to find it out for yourself. In literary parlance, this may be called "fractured structure."

While it is true that the country referred to in *Shame* could be any country that has been ruined by dictatorship and political corruption, the exact setting – Pakistan – needs to be identified because that geographical and historical specificity is what makes it a novel and not a mere political allegory on dictatorships.

The main lines are clear enough, for names and events are rather thinly veiled, unlike the heavy burqa of its women. At one level, *Shame* is the story of Isky Harappa (Zulfikar Ali Bhutto) and Raza Hyder (Zia), two presidents of Pakistan; it is the story of how Bhutto, seeking to perpetuate his power by keeping the army in his pocket, appointed "the most incompetent general" as commander-in-chief so that he need not fear insubordination or an army take-over. But "the idea that a general is likely to remain in your pocket . . . is .a very stupid and dangerous idea" *(Kunapipi, 14).* Zia ousted Bhutto, had him hanged, and set up a regime of religious bigotry. Benazir Bhutto is very like Arjumand Harappa who adored her father, and Rushdie's *Shame (1983)* foretells the rise and return of Benazir Bhutto (126). It would be an interesting exercise to trace the real life sequel to the Isky-Raza story.

Within the Isky-Raza story, Rushdie packs an arsenal of satire: indiscriminate and groundless police arrests (by Talvar ul Haq, the whole name ironically stands translated as sword in defence of the faith); the farce of elections where recounts of ballots set right those results which earlier coercion had failed to bring in line (178); Raza's Gichki-Needle Valley ruthlessness (102-104); Haroun Harappa's rich-boy tantrums *(Shame* 147-150); bribery as part of Customs Officers' lives (51); Isky's "diplomatic" persecution of Soviet and American ambassadors (185) being some of the notable episodes.

Rushdie also uses authorial intrusions to comment on specific social and political ills: the long joke about Zia's deal with God (112); a comment on Islamic fundamentalism being imposed from government levels (251); an interlude on various aspects of everyday life in Pakistan (68-69); all these could be illustrated with historical examples.

There are also numerous references to specific people and events; as with the Sabarmati episode in *Midnight's Children,* though not much is lost for posterity if it does not relate it to the actual Nanavati case but takes it as a narrative device to further Saleem's reaction to his aunt's affair, not much is lost if future readers are ignorant of such details in recent Pakistani history; however, contemporary scholarship could catalogue this type of information more easily than future scholarship since it is more readily accessible now. Hyder's (Major Zia's) conquest of Aansu ka Wadi in 1947-48 (79), Prime Minister Liaquat Ali Khan's assassination in October 1951, (81) Isky's (Bhutto's) trail (227), all are landmarks in real history – and an authentic background to each of these numerous historical allusions enriches the characterisation of the people in *Shame.*

More significant and useful would be yet another facet of background documentation: notes on linguistic and cultural references in the novel. An associate, who knows I am working on a full-length study of Rushdie, suggested that we compile a glossary as part of our work. I baulked at this initially, for I believe that a good writer usually weaves the meaning of foreign phrases and cultural allusions into his narrative, that a glossary is already there for a conscientious reader to pick up. But some of the current scholarship on Rushdie reveals that the history and culture of the Indian subcontinent are, perhaps, too complex for the western reader. Therefore, though an explicatory approach might seem rather rudimentary, it is perhaps necessary, for even the simplest events in history need to be set straight for the outsiders.

For example, Robert L. Ross in his essay on Partition novels from India and Pakistan quotes Javid Iqbal's arguments for Muslims' desire for Partition: "and secondly because they desired to develop themselves on the line of their own distinctive culture" (Ross, 63).

He then adds a statement of his own: "The Hindus, in a like manner, wanted; to pursue a culture derived from their own equally distinctive religious identity."

The latter statement is blatantly erroneous. Only one of the political groups, other than the. Muslim League, wanted Partition on religious grounds, and it (R.S:S.) was not a major power-bloc. The Congress and other groups wanted a secular country, and politically India has remained secular even in times of bloodiest communal riots. In sheer numbers, there are twice as many Muslims in India today as there were in undivided India and the ratio of Muslims to Hindus has surpassed that of undivided India within two decades of Partition despite the mass exodus of Muslims in 1947.

Ross's statement seems a harmless and trivial lapse but these innocuous bits of disinformation (that marvellous word of the 1980s) tend to get repeated and proliferated and before we realise it, a whole generation of students accept and perpetuate the disinformation.

Perhaps I seem overzealous about this point, but I happen to live in Canada where disinformation about the religious distinctions in the Indian community has led to a tacit assumption by government and public that the Sikhs are a separate entity from all others of Indian origin. This ignores the reality, which is that each regional culture is about as similar or different from any other regional culture within India and that culture, religion and politics are perceived quite differently by insiders on the one hand and outsiders on the other.

The quarrel over insiders and outsiders exists in Commonwealth Literary Criticism as well and is an unending and indecisive one. Critics have argued that Rushdie himself is an outsider. David Edgar, reviewing *Shame,* says it is written "from the outside . . . by a British resident and fits subject matter is a country to which the author is only a visitor." Rukmini Bhaya Nair answers Edgar by saying that Saleem and Omar Khayyam "though homegrown, do share his alien system of values." She thus places author and narrators in the *same* cell but *outside* the society which is the subject of the novels. I would place author and narrators in the *same cell* but *within* the society of which they write.

A good writer, especially one who adopts the comic or satiric mode, gets "inside" through personal knowledge, instinct or conscientious homework. Given the evidence of Rushdie's novels and his journalistic *(The Jaguar Smile)* and critical output (he writes articles and reviews books regularly for English newspapers) I would say Rushdie's expertise about India and Pakistan comes from a combination of all three factors. However, they are not in the same ratio, the "novelist's instinct" takes the largest share in the mixture. Writers are often blessed with serendipity, and perhaps would do well to realise that it is a gift and not to be explained. Indeed, the less writers talk about their work the greater its effectiveness (Faulkner was one of the rare novelists who kept away from interviews); and the less critics listen to writers talking about their own work the more effective their interpretation is likely to be. To give just one example of this, Rushdie's use of the Shiva-Parvati-Ganesh allusion in *Midnight's Children is* just right in many ways, though, admittedly, there is some crudity in Shiva's military and sexual exploits. The mythic dimension though clearly implied is kept in the background while the real characters are larger than life in the foreground. The readers make their own connections at the level of associative networks, subcutaneous experiences so to say; the critics might give their own interpretive slant and hammer it home with pedagogical zeal but fellow-critics know where the line of explication ends and of opinion begins; besides, the more numerous the interpretations, the richer the experience of scholarship. But once the writer states something, even though the discerning reader knows that the writer is only one of the critics once he has written – the final line of his novel, some configurations change. This is what happens when we read Rushdie state in an interview,

> The legend of Ganesh is the legend of disputed parentage . . . . Shiva becomes convinced that his wife has been fooling around, that this child is not his ... Now it seemed to me that since Saleem's entire ancestry is also very murky and disputed . . . it was correct to give him, as a mythological ancestor, somebody with disputed ancestry, with a disputed family line *(Kunapipi, 91).*

Even aside from the mysterious inversion here that makes Saleem himself a Ganesha-figure instead of making him the Siva-figure in the above version of the myth, the quotation

(a) limits the reader's experience to just one aspect of the whole myth,

(b) indicates that Rushdie, either knowingly or in half-knowledge, distorts the original version by using a folk version (another example of disinformation) and this makes us question his competence and/or motivation (what would an outsider, a Muslim, know about Hinduism, or has he internationally spoofed a story held in reverence by Hindus?) and

(c) generally diverts us into extraneous considerations such as the one just given.

A mythic archetype works precisely because of its multi-dimensional richness, its central axle from which radiate numerous spokes of versions, associations and side-products that extend to form the wheel that is the novel. If I were to write a novel using this Puranic story, it might be to show that marriage is an equal partnership and that the child of an equal partner is equal to a child of the other partner, and indeed both child and the married pair have rights arid responsibilities to one another regardless of details of conception or fertilisation. But whatever my interpretation, I would be wise to restrain myself from imposing my version as the original Puranic version in an interview!

Given Rushdie's statement, a critical study could explore yet another avenue: of how, despite his own conscious unfamiliarity, the author has hit upon very effective mythic references, for example, in his choice of Parvati and Padma in *Midnight's Children,* and of Maulana Dawood and Sufiya Zinobia in *Shame.* The relevant point in all this would or should be the *effect of* allusions rather than their origin, though authentic explication of origins should be part of a definitive study.

Of the numerous patterns that an overview, of the labyrinth gives us, there is one that intrigues me because of the brilliance of its intricate craftsmanship. This is Rushdie's method of stretching an allusion or reference to its limit and beyond. As mentioned earlier, there are two analogies that come to mind-of a singer stretching a note on the breath that seems endless and of a glassblower shaping glass into incredibly elaborate coils and shapes in one continuous movement. Both artists often give yet another dexterous twist at the very end before letting the note or glass taper off into its own space.

In *Shame,* this stretching recurs often and in diverse ways. But the important factor to note is that the starting point for each of these marvellous pyrotechnics is the solid reality of something very familiar.

The "stretching" is done in three main ways: a continuing metaphor is formulated land intermittently stretched through the rest of the novel; a reference is used only once but is stretched within the context to its limit, and it might or might not imply a metaphor; and then there are what seem to be totally bizarre things or events stretched onto the edge of credibility. To consider just one example of each, there are: the continuing métaphor of an upside-down world; the den of the forty thieves; and the dumb waiter: All three of these examples occur early enough in the narrative to lead the reader into an awareness of this technique as essential to the novel.

Omar Khayyam Shakil's first view of the world is of the upside down dumb-bell shaped mountains of Q because he was held upside down, as most babies are as soon as they are born to let mucus and fluids gravitate downwards and let lungs start functioning. This perfectly natural and familiar event is the starting point for a series of events through the novel that stretch this idea of inversion. Like the perforated sheet in *Midnight's Children,* a custom becomes a metaphor. Shakil's world is upside down and later the novel stresses yet another aspect of this – his view of the world is upside down. Thus, in childhood his world is an inversion of the usual fairy-tale world. Instead of the usual parent-and-three-children storyline *(Cinderella),* we get three mothers and a child; instead of a tyrannical ogre we get three too-loving mothers; and later, instead of a prince rescuing a princess from a tower, we have Shakil joining his wife in a tower. As in fairy tales people get married, but they never ever live happily ever after.

However, beyond the literal inversions lies one of the central metaphors of the novel – the country that is the subject of the novel is both victim and perpetrator of – an inverted vision of life. At Partition, the original inhabitants of the land were driven to the background and

> it was the ones who were really new, the distant cousins and half acquaintances and total strangers who poured in from the east . . . who took over and got things done (81).

The new history was written by *mohajirs,* the immigrants from India, whose vision naturally had violence, aggressiveness and bitterness and they displaced the leisurely pace and continuity of the old way of life.

While these aspects of upside-downness are consistently developed, there are also numerous minor references to inversion, obtuse as in the younger sister getting married before the elder or contrived, or built up step by step and summed up as in the narrator's description of Bilquis:

> As a woman who was unclothed by change but who wrapped herself in certainties . . . or as that lady whose father was a Woman and whose son turned out to be a girl as well; and whose man of men . . . was himself obliged, in the end, to 'put on the humiliating black shroud of womanhood. (67-68)

The total effect of these inversions is cumulative. Though singly, each reference or episode is funny or satirical or poignant, the cumulative, experience is one of extreme pessimism about the present and future *of* the country where everything is upside down.

The stretching of a realistic reference to its extreme is also seen in single references such as the episode of the den of forty thieves. Bariamma's house is a "forest of new relatives," "a bloodjungle" where Bilquis has to share a "cavernous bedroom" with forty other female relatives. Rushdie's description of the husbands' stealthy entry and lovemaking seems unadulterated fantasy but it is only an exaggeration of a joint-family set-up and not fabrication. Attia Hosain's sensitive and realistic novel, *Sunlight on a Broken Column,* also refers to such a dormitory set-up on a terrace. The same is true of the Harappa house. In the "backyard of the universe" in Sind, the Harappa mansion is furnished with the opulence of decades – paintings framed in gilt, Sheraton chairs, cut-glass decanters and thick carpets. Similarly, the Raza household with its attic suite where Sufiya lived, a princess in the tower, watched over by her nurse and her husband, is also based in reality for it was not only in Sherlock Holmes and Bronte that the unwanted members of the family were kept imprisoned out of sight.

However, in each case, the realistic base is stretched beyond its utmost. Bariamma's house is an exaggeration of the joint-family set-up that is, or was, fairly standard practice especially in a traditional way of life: Instead of the three or four couples that shared a house, we have forty. Like teenage girls, the forty have a chaperone, Bariamrma who, like a good chaperone looks the other way so her "girls" can have some fun. Her loud snores are a signal for them to enter, and once the last of them leaves, she stops snoring. The stretching goes further. That sex is a private activity is taken to its extreme, of total negation that altogether obliterates the act so that when pregnancies occurred they did so as if by magic, as if all conceptions were immaculate and all births virgin (74).

There is a further negation of the concept of "purity" (Pakistan, Land of the Pure) and privacy. For clearly, far from the sexual abstinence implied in the dormitory set-up, it could be "just the excuse for the biggest orgy on earth" for "who would know if her real husband had come to her? And who would complain?" (73)

In Rushdie, there are metaphors lurking at every turn. Like Bilquis, he is "scarcely capable of speaking except in metaphors" (208). Bariamrna's zenana is a metaphor for several statements. It satirises the hypocrisy of "bourgeois morality" to use Shavian Dolittle's phrase. More importantly, it is a metaphor for the society delineated in *Shame, a* country where "there is a kind of Gogolian system where the ruling class is minute and politics is a kind of family quarrel" *(Kunapipi,* 18) and in which "there are only temporary alliances based on mutual self-interest" (209).

There are two other dimensions to the metaphor. In the political context, in this fertile and cavernous bedroom, Bilquis and Raza alone "cannot make them [children] here, in this zoo, like they all do" (85). In the social and political context, Rushdie is brilliantly insightful about the way family-sense is nurtured. Referring to the telling and retelling of the story of how Bilquis, clad only in her muslin *dupatta,* was rescued by Raza, the narrator says:

> because stories, such stories were the glue that held the clan together, binding the generations in webs of whispered secrets (76).

At the personal and political level, the webs of whispered secrets dictate the course of events.

The third kind of stretching of fact into the fantastic is exemplified in the dumb waiter. The realistic base is probably: the scaffolding that is erected in building construction; it could also be quite literally the dumb waiter of restaurants, as in Pinter's play *The Dumb Waiter.* In shutting themselves from the world, the Shakil sisters could have devised the dumb waiter as the equivalent of Rapunzel's hair in the fairy tale. The device in itself is consistent with the tone of the opening chapter and though it is little more than a game to speculate the sequence of the novel's development, it seems as though the finer details were reworked after the novel-ending took place. The structure is rather realistically assembled, however fantastic the concept behind it. It is large, enough to hold "three grown adults." At this point in the story it seems a foreshadowing of the death of the three sisters. It is a defence "against intruders," and clearly a system whereby the inmates could get provisions transported. It is built "in such a way that it could be operated without requiring the mansion's inhabitants to show themselves." Then the image is gradually stretched so that each step links plausibly with the preceding: one, from winches to inside switch to secret panels with eighteen inch stiletto blades "sharp sharp." It is perhaps because this last was added after the story reached its gruesome climax that the stiletto blades are "sharp sharp" without getting rusted in the sixty odd years between its genesis and its final ghastly utility to chop up Raza's body.

The evolution of a string of events or characteristics, each linked within limits of plausibility to the preceding is one of the dexterous techniques employed in the novel, so that, though the first which is obviously factual bears little resemblance to the last which seems as clearly fantastical, the spun-glass line of continuity is clear when one studies it. The most brilliant use of this technique is seen in Sufiya Zinobia's "blushing." The factual basis of sensitive baby-skin is gradually stretched through physical, events into its emotional counterparts until Sufiya's over-sensitive skin changes into an emotional mainspring of shame which, stretched to its limits, erupts into volcanic violence and destruction.

Sufiya Zenobia is, as the narrator keeps insisting, the main character This brings me to the fourth point mentioned at the beginning: the fractured structure of the novel, or is it only seemingly fractured?

Elsewhere (Parameswaran, 1988) I have argued that *Shame is* architecturally imbalanced because one of its supporting or foundation pillars – the Isky-Raza story is in the satiric mode and the other – the Shakil-Sufiya story is in the fantastic mode, and the cross-beam between the two consists of contrived events. However, it is worth speculating whether there is a way of reconciling these; whether the two circuits in the labyrinth are functional to the structure; whether it is not after all the writer's prerogative to paint two sides of his Rubik's cube in the same colour.

Sufiya is the embodiment of shame and Shakil of shamelessness. Shakil's shamelessness is developed only peripherally but Sufiya's sense of shame permeates all aspects of the novel. Rushdie's authorial comments show the genesis of the novel (115-118). Sufiya is the fusion of three figures: a Pakistani girl killed by her father for her love-affair with a white boy; a boy in a newspaper report who apparently ignited himself without any external fuel or flame; and an imaginary girl conjured up by Rushdie's musings on subway assaults, who, unlike other victims, springs back on her attackers in a frenzy of strength and tears them limb from limb.

> Humiliate people for long enough and a wildness bursts out of them (117).

Sufiya can be likened to the spirit of Pakistan blushing at the indignities heaped upon her by her own kith and kin who had expected her to be something other than she was and who turns out to be, because of their actions and attitudes, wild, the Beast within breaking out of her. Her lack of mental development, and her emotional instability could well be Rushdie's statement on Pakistan.

Rushdie plays on various dichotomies in the novel and draws each to its extreme evolution. For example, Isky and Raza are opposites; tear-ridden Raza with his grandiose ambitions of fathering a warrior, evolves into a religious fanatic; and debonair, hedonistic Isky evolves into an ambitious dictator. The basic dichotomy is part of the history of the land – the civilisations of Mohenjo-Daro and Harappa are said to have been polarised opposites, and certainly the opulent and aesthete culture of the great Moghuls was very different from the puritanical abstinence preached by orthodox Islam and imposed by Aurangzeb, and more recently by Ayatollah Khomeini and his ilk.

Sufiya is the embodiment of this dualism, the beauty within the beast alternating with the beast within the beauty. Rushdie's handling of characterisation is superb in the scene where Suflya plays with the toys in her head (213) and we cannot but be compassionate with this beautiful-child within the beast that has so recently decapitated two hundred and eighteen turkeys, and will in her own time decapitate her husband who had never been husband. Whether or not Sufiya herself recognises how she has been betrayed by all around her, we can. And in this way, Sufiya becomes the personification not only of Pakistan, not only of all countries where the political climate is conducive to dictatorship but of the duality of the human condition, the duality of being both victim and perpetrator of violence.

## Works Cited

David Edgar, "The Migrant's Vision" *New Left Review, 144* (March-April 1981). *2. Kunapipi Vol. VII, No.* 1, 1985 (An Interview with Salman Rushdie).

Rukmini Bhaya Nair, "The Voyeur's View in *Midnight's Children* and *Shame*". *ACLALS Bulletin,* 7th Series.1,1985.

Uma Parameswaran, *The Perforated Sheet: Essays on Salman Rushdie's Art* Madras: Affiliated East-West Press, 1988.

Robert L. Ross, "The Emerging Myth: Partition in the Indian and Pakistanian (sic) Novel," *ACLALS Bulletin,* 7th Series, No. 4, 1986.

Salman Rushdie, *Shame.* London: Picador, 1984 (first published 1983).

# 10

# Impressive Women but the Chains are no Fictions

## Women in Rushdie's *Shame*

Salman Rushdie is an ardent crusader of women's rights and strengths. He delineates the freedoms and oppressions faced by women in their traditional roles, and portrays a diversity of strong women who make their own space, and reach out for controlling their own destinies sometimes despite and sometimes because of traditional codes of conduct. No sooner than I type these words onto the computer screen than other voices jam the system clamouring to be heard.

He is what's-its-name a doubledyed chauvinist, look how he uses women as sex objects and nothing but, look at Jocasta, Pinkie Aurangzeb and Farah the Parsee.

That's right; and a racist to boot, charging Parsees with unbridled sexuality, poor Shahbanou.

Racist all right, denying his own race, country and religion, desecrating women right left and centre, stripping Bilquis nude

---

This was written by invitation in 1992, and the volume appeared in 1998: *Women in Indo-Anglian Fiction: Tradition and Modernity*. Ed. Naresh K. Jain. New Delhi: Manohar. 1998. pp. 141-157.

to her dupatta and stretching his filthy hand even to the lives of the Prophet, upon whom be peace. Racist pig. . .

Bloody brown sahib is what. So why doesn't he ever say anything against Christianity huh? or Judaism? Always coming down on eastern religions, giving goddess names to Padma and Parvati, illiterates and magicians. . .

If we were to tabulate a case history of Mr. Rushdie and take cognizance of the inter-relatedness of his fiction with his own life and training in the West since the age of fourteen, it would not be illogical to deduce that the dysfunctional family syndrome that we see in his fiction is symptomatic of larger problems at the personal and ethnocultural levels.

As an avant-garde intellectual, it is not at all surprising that Rushdie should project the Lacanian paradigm of the conflict between the imaginary state of bonding with the mother and the symbolic state of developed consciousness. The situation becomes more complex when one sees that the process of individuation is hindered by cultural repressions.

Is there a single person in his novels who is plain and simple faithful to the spouse?

Or any scene saying hallelujah to plainandsimple marital love? Always perverted, always and only brutish carnal cavorting, shame shame.

Who he thinks he is? How he can know anything about parents' love and Shakil Sisters' mourning for their son? Poking fun at old people, Reverend Mother and Bariamma and Dolores O'Toole, so what if god gives one a moustache, another baldness or a humpback?

Exactly, god makes some children empty in the breadbin as Bilquis says; so who is Salman to drag poor Sufiya and Toxy Catrack for all the world to see?

The voices go on, more insistent than the radio waves set up by Midnight's children.

One could retract the first line of the first paragraph and go on to substantiate all the rest and prove that what's-its-name is a doubledyed male chauvinist. Given the excesses of sexual acrobatics in *Grimus*, and Padma's preoccupation with Saleem's 'other pencil', and the much publicized polemics of the brothel in

*The Satanic Verses*, it will not be too difficult to advance an argument that women are trivialized and exaggeratedly sexualized.

Or, one could erase all but the first line and bring forward Robert Graves and Leslie Fiedler, Edward Said and Jacques Lacan, Derrida and Kristeva, to show that Rushdie is indeed weaving patterns mythic, historical, anticolonial, psychoanalytic, deconstructionist, semiotic – which delineate women with an authenticity of detail that characterizes Rani Humayun's eighteen shawls.

This route is tempting, for these are contemporary criticism's gods and one must pay due homage to these outer shrines before entering the inner shrine where cultural sensitivity and common sense are the perambulatory paths to a more down-to-earth form of appreciating the sculpted beauty of the text against life as lived rather than as dissected by literary pundits. However, in the present context of tradition and modernity, it is practical to restrict oneself to one of the other shrines – The White Goddess.

Graves, in *The White Goddess*, divides women into three mythological representations: Diana, virgin goddess; Venus, goddess of love, sex and fertility; and Hecate, goddess of death and oracles. The White-Goddess is all three; she is the Moon in its three phases New, Full and Waning. Graves traces how all ancient cultures had the same central concept of the triple female identity that represented the three phases of youth, maturity and decay in Nature's cycle. He quotes from Apuleius' vision of the Queen of Heaven who reveals herself to be Ceres, Diana, Minerva, Proserpine, Juno, Hecate and indeed mother of all creation.

The concept of the Triple Goddess, as feminist critics such as Mary Daly have discussed, was present in all ancient cultures, but was displaced in each by patriarchy. Daly summarizes the identity of the Triple Goddess in various ancient religions: Hera-Demeter-Kore of pre-Hellenic times, Thetis, Amphitrite, Nereis of Hellenic mythology, Neith triple Goddess of Libya, Eire, Phodla, Banbha of Ireland, and Myrine who was mother of the gods in Phrygian lore. In Hinduism, Parvati, Lakshmi and Sarasvati could be the equivalent rather than the parallel of the

White Goddess, in that they are the triple deity but do not correspond to virgin, lover and crone but to three traits fundamental to continuity of culture and civilization, namely, creativity, progress, and transmission of cumulative knowledge.

In Rushdie's fiction, we see the Triple Goddess vindicated both in individuals and as principle. As individual, we see her in Naseem Ghani-Mrs. Aadam Aziz-Reverend Mother, changing from virginal goddess to be adored through a white perforated sheet in snow-covered Kashmir, to Venus and Ceres running a household of five children, husband and servants in Agra, to Hecate presiding over the Sinai household in Bombay. We see the Triple Goddess phases in Amina though she is never as dominant in any stage as Naseem. We see her in a perverted but identifiable form in Kamala Sutra Media-Livia/Jocasta in *Grimus*.

As principle, Graves' White Goddess is present in *The Satanic Verses*. Lat, Uzza and Manat 'are the exalted birds, and their intercession is desired indeed' (p.114). In *The Serpent and the Rope,* Raja Rao's Rama says that Catholicism became a universal religion once the Mother of God replaced the Son of Man. So it is with Jahilia's new religion in *The Satanic Verses.* Rushdie recognizes this human need for the goddess; as soon as Mahound pays tribute to the patron deities of the town, Grandee Abu Simbel and Hind accept his new faith, and the populace follows their lead:

> both the crowd in the tent and the overflow of men and women outside it, begins to kneel, row by row, the movement rippling outwards from Hind and the Grandee as though they were pebbles thrown into a lake. *(SV, 115)*

The homage of Abu Simbel and Hind is motivated by politics but the crowd's homage is only partly dictated by the political powers of the day; they bow down because the new religion combined the best of the old tenets and infused new blood. Their goddesses were Allah's daughters. That history took a wrong turn in ousting the goddesses is another story.

The traditional *burqa,* that covers women from top to toe, is in a way symbolic of the banishment of the goddesses from human sight. In Rushdie, the *burqa is a* touchstone of the measure of one's negative traditionalism. One of the first rules that

Aadam Aziz lays down to his wife is that she give up purdah. Culturally indoctrinated into certain ideas of what constitutes immodesty, Naseem reacts with dismay: "You want me to walk naked in front of strange men." When he argues that her dress covers everything but her face and feet, she cries, "They will see more than that! They will see my deep-deep shame!'(*MNC*, 34) Aadam's mother had shed her *burqa* even earlier, rising to the exigencies of being a businesswoman. Both women quickly shed a tradition and enter modernity. For the women of *Shame*, it is not so easy to step out of figurative purdah whether or not they wear a *burqa*. However, despite their traditional handicap, they strike out for a certain measure of identity and independence.

Rushdie recognizes the strength there is in women and also the force of the chains that bind them. His women characters are strong and individualistic. They take over whatever space they are in; even if it is as narrow as the single bed on which Sufiya Zinobia sleeps, it is theirs and woe to the one who dares encroach on their personal space. Of this takeover, the author says in *Shame*:

> I had thought, before I began, that what I had on my hands was an almost excessively masculine tale, a saga of sexual rivalry, ambition, power, patronage, betrayal, death, revenge. But the women seem to have taken over; they marched in from the peripheries of the story to demand the inclusion of their own tragedies, histories and comedies . . . It occurs to me that the women knew precisely what they were up to-that their stories explain, and even subsume, the men's. (*S*, 173)

He goes on to say:

> it goes without saying that not all woman are crushed by any system, no matter how oppressive. It is commonly, and I believe accurately, said of Pakistan that her women are much more impressive than her men.... Their chains, nevertheless, are no fictions. (*S*, 173)

These statements might well form the core of any study of Rushdie's delineation of women.

It is noteworthy that Rushdie uses the pronoun 'her' for Pakistan. This might be merely due to the translation involved from Urdu to English, assuming that the 'common' saying would be in the vernacular. However, since this is the only place where Pakistan is personified and given a gender, it should be taken as significant. Despite Rushdie's impatience at Indians' propensity to confer allegory on literary creations (interview in *Kunapipi*) Pakistan has to be seen as a woman ravaged by an all-male domination. Like Bilquis, Pakistan 'was unclothed by change, but . . . wrapped herself in certainties' (S, 67) and in an existential sense, certainties are deceptive. Arjumand Harappa, contemptuous of her sex as many abused women are, rejects it, trains herself to be masculine, and joins the patriarchal group to the further abuse of the country. But Rushdie is right in disapproving of allegorical readings in that allegories tend to universalize situations and to distance the reader from the personal experiences of the characters as individuals. As Margaret Atwood says in *Survival,* victimization can conveniently be adduced to a 'necessity decreed by History; or Economics, or the Unconscious, or any other large general powerful idea' (*Survival,* 37).

Atwood's four basic victim positions – denial, explaining away as defined above, a will to change the situation, and being a 'creative non-victim' might be an appropriate chart by which to categorize Rushdie's women characters. However, as with the White Goddess paradigm, this will be restrictive. Neither in real life, nor in Rushdie, are women to be compartmentalized into one or other pigeon-hole. A more aesthetically productive approach would be to see them as living breathing women moving against the backdrop of a traditional culture that itself is continually evolving.

'Tradition' is an elusive word that defies definition because it ignites instant value judgements; some think of it as sacrosanct, others as hollow idols that must be thrown out. Moreover, different cultures superimpose their own value systems on other cultures; this is particularly dangerous in the light of Western critical imperialism which might see the Indian, Pakistani and Arab cultures delineated in Rushdie's novels as totally benighted and steeped in outdated oppressive 'traditionalism'. To confuse matters still further, there is some relevance to one of the imaginary voices quoted above – that Rushdie's intellectual make-up has been shaped by the West. Armed with the caveats, it is time to meet the women in *Shame,* and consider how each reacts to tradition and modernity. Each one's attitude towards certain key facets of tradition and modernity might yield relevant patterns. One could list certain items on this hypothetical questionnaire: attitude to gender-role expectations in appearance, social behaviour, speech habits, marriage, faithfulness in marriage, parental obligations, personal fulfilment and ambitions.

There are two distinct classes of people in the vertical hierarchy of society that forms the setting of the novel. Most of the minor women characters belong to the working classes, and the major characters to an affluent aristocracy. Rushdie eschews the middle class. None of the women is ever seen working in the kitchen or worrying about ration lines or school admission for children, though we are told that Bilquis ran her father's house and was given 'slightly more than her fair share of household duties' in the Bariamma household (*S,* 75). Rushdie excuses himself by saying this is not a realistic novel (*S,* 69) but in many ways it is. It gives a very authentic picture of women caught between the freedoms and oppressions of both, tradition and modernity.

Among the minor women characters are those of the town of Q, Zeenat Kabuli and Farida Balloch, and those of the city – Duniyazad Begum. These women are stereotypically traditional but we remember their brief appearance because of the exuberance of their hatred. Zeenat and Farida ensure that Maulana Dawood does not snatch always their hour with his colourful curses; Duniyazad, a cousin in the Bariamma household, flings the most hurtful of all traditional taunts at Bilquis, that of barrenness, and the public fistfight that follows leaves clumps of hair and broken tooth on the dormitory floor.

Among other minor characters are the ayahs, or caregivers in current terminology – Hashmat Bibi in Q., Isky's nameless ayah in Mohenjo, and Shahbanou in the city. All three can be seen as stereotypically traditional domestics, totally devoted to their employers. Hashmat Bibi serves the Shakil sisters and their father, ministering to their material needs; Isky's ayah adores him, 'fawning over Iskander as if her were three years old, or a deity, or both' (*S*, 108); Shahbanou is more enigmatic. Her dedication far surpasses the bounds of duty and she ministers to Shakil's physical needs as well as Sufiya's material needs. In this, is she being traditional or modernist? Traditional in that she sacrifices herself in lieu of her mistress whom she genuinely loves, or modernist in being pragmatic about keeping Shakil's health under control, knowing that 'it is only a matter of time before you lose control or burst' (*S*, 211). One would think that these are the two ways of reading her motivation; but a third view, that emerged from a discussion with a friend, is that Shahbanou might just be satisfying her own needs. I do not quite see where the text implies this but I insert this in passing as an example of cross-cultural dialogue. Paul de Man speaks of 'misreading'. A good misreading is 'a text that produces another text which can itself be shown to be an interesting misreading' (DeMann, 51). A misreading turns a work inside out, reverses the traditional reading to reveal layers that are hidden. Perhaps, my reading of Rushdie's women as strong, individualistic characters who make their own space despite great odds is such a creative misreading!

The major characters are Bilquis Hyder and Rani Harappa in the city and the Shakil sisters in Q. Dichotomy and pairs abound in Rushdie. The Shakil household parallels and contrasts the Bariamma household. Both are patterned on a form of traditional autocracy but the contrasts are gendered and through this gendering, Rushdie shows his appreciation of women's strengths. The first is dominated by a patriarch and the second by a matriarch. Whereas the oppression of the first is unmitigated, the oppressions of the second are mixed with a variety of positive qualities. Despite fearing and hating their father, the Shakil sisters end up imitating his arrogance (which ignores and thus alienates the local elite) and his heretical fanaticism (Omar comes into the world 'without benefit of mutilation, barbery or divine approval') and his unrepentant egotism. Arjumand is another product of a father-dominated family.

Given the recurrence of unloving and unlovable, unforgiving and unforgivable fathers in Rushdie's fiction, one might be tempted to say it is an autobiographical component, but given his positive treatment of women, it might be pertinent to hold that Rushdie is distinguishing between male-dominated traditions and female dominated traditions.

While father-dominated Shakil sisters replicate their father's evil in themselves, the women under Bariamma's rule, even while fearing and hating the domineering matriarch, end up being influenced only by her good qualities, of which she has several, unlike old Shakil who has none. Tradition has much to give to contemporary life, and the sense of family that Bariamma nurtures is one of its positive contributions.

While it is easy to argue that the Bariamma house is traditional and that Bilquis strikes out for modernity by insisting on leaving it, one most ensure that it is understood that the dormitory is Rushdie's exaggerated and extended satire on the joint-family system. Rushdie himself is careful to point out one positive aspect of the system: it promotes a sense of family. A.K. Ramanujan has a poem where the speaker says to his wife, "Really what keeps us apart/at the end of years is unshared/ childhood" and thinks, even if facetiously, of the wisdom in the old custom of child marriages which would have "wed us in the oral cradle".

In Bariamma's realm, each newcomer was brought into the oral cradle. Family stories, Rushdie says, were the glue that held the clan together, binding the generations in webs of whispered secrets. After several additions and deletions, when Bilquis' story of her rescue by Raza settled down into hallowed text, Bilquis knew that she had become a member of the family: 'in the sanctification of her text lay initiation, kinship, blood' (S, 76-77).

The family as centre was integral to the traditional culture of the subcontinent. Rushdie has said that he sees the leadership of Pakistan, and other dictatorships, as revolving around family cliques, and therefore the analogy fits at the literal and figurative levels. It is significant at both levels that the extended family is quickly reduced to three nuclear families-those of Isky, Raza and Mir. Even as it has all but vanished from contemporary life, the Bariamma model of family vanished with time within the novel. Of the forty thieves and their partners, only two pairs continued their interaction – Bilquis-Raza and Rani-Isky. Bilquis, Raza and

Rani are from mother-figure dominated families. Though Bilquis is brought up by her father, he is called Mahmoud the Woman because of his lack of aggressiveness and therefore Bilquis can be said to have the same background as Rani who grows up under Bariamma's tutelage.

Bilquis and Rani have conventional dreams of getting out of a confined environment and becoming queens by virtue of marrying a prince. To invert the fairy tale archetype, they expect to be transformed from moth to butterfly, from frog to princess as soon as the designated prince kisses them. Bilquis is chosen by Raza whereas Rani's marriage is arranged in a conventional manner; but both have the same partly romanticized, partly passive attitude to marriage. Both enjoy love-making and seem to be fully satisfied and fully to satisfy their husbands. But married life changes a woman's course even in the most harmonious of unions, and for these two it changes drastically because of their husbands' political ambitions. Isky peremptorily silences Rani when she, lulled with her first lovemaking, speaks of his companion, the doctor that 'everybody in town is calling such a bad influence on you' (*S*, 80). This is an omen of what is to come in their future together. Isky will go his way and Rani must draw from whatever inner strengths family and genes have given her. Similarly, Bilquis' future with Raza is foretold in her beginning. Rescued during pre-partition riots, wooed with gifts from plundered booty, she starts her wedded life as a nomadic soldier's wife and ends it that way, though Raza at some point became primarily a soldier of Islam.

Both Bilquis and Rani are left alone for long periods of time by their husbands. Their friendship realistically shows the bond that often develops between women. They candidly share secrets and hopes in the Diana phase; they brag about their spouse's sexual prowess and their pastimes in the Venus phase; they can be quite cattish as seen in Bilquis retailing tidbits of gossip over the phone about Isky's philandering; but there is a bond between them that withstands their husband's bitter rivalries. The bond is due to the traditions they share and not due to similarities in character because they are very different.

They react differently to similar situations. When Rani hears of Isky's affair with Mir's woman, she continues to embroider, keeping her anger under control with regality, and in time becomes as formidable a figure as Dickens' Mme. Defarge; when on the other hand Bilquis is told of Raza's unsuccessful wooing of Pinkie, she takes the comment as an insult and forces Raza to consider it as a matter of besmirched honour. When forced into grass-widowhood by their husbands' absence, Rani takes recourse to embroidering her anger into her shawls whereas Bilquis has an affair with Sindbad Mengal, who is, ironically, a cinema man like her father. When their world turns topsy turvy around them, Rani withdraws into herself, both at the time of Mir's raid on Mohenjo and when placed under house arrest; but Bilquis loses her mental balance. The loo wind symbolizes change for Bilquis and she is terrified of it. Rani holds her own to the very end. Both are almost vengefully faithful to their spouses towards the end. Rani skillfully manoeuvers to find out that Isky had been murdered before being hanged, and Bilquis engineers Raza's escape from his house before Armageddon.

Bilquis, who yearned for fixities, is driven from Delhi to Karachi to Quetta and finally dies a horrible death. Her wedded life ends as it began, in flight but also with commitment to each other. Rushdie has little sympathy for Raza and the man he represents in real life, but as a good writer he has inscribed patterns perhaps despite himself. Raza might be a stupid dictator advised by a vengeful fanatic (Dawood); he might have been blinded by his desire for a son to the point of being traumatizingly cruel to his newborn daughter; but there are moments of infinite tenderness in him. For example, when he carries Sufiya in his arms after she has decapitated Pinkie's turkeys; when at Naveed's funeral he looks at Bilquis and sees her 'history as a slow retreat from that early nudity into the secrecy of the veil' and murmurs, 'Ah Bilquis, what happened to our lives?' (*S*, 228); and most poignantly, when he finds Bilquis in the far room of the Shakil dungeons:

> "Don't *worry, Billoo"*, he whispered to her, "Raz is here. *I'll* clean you up good and proper and then you'll see . . .

What's the meaning of this, you're not supposed to die? *(S, 280)*

Raza is to a great extent, a scion of Bariamma's matriarchal mould, after all. Through the reference to the *burqa* image and the decay of love between Raza and Bilquis, Rushdie communicates both the failure of Pakistan and the sadness of women's plight as the country regressed into a religious dictatorship.

Both Bilquis and Rani are more sinned against than sinning. We empathize with their limited options and their essential humanity. We admire Rushdie for his sensitive portrayal of their aspirations and the unjust suffering forced on them by their husbands' ambitions and infidelities. Having Rani Harappa sign her shawls as Rani Humayun is a fine touch of inscribing identity on one who deserved it.

Rushdie makes ironical use of setting and of choice of names to trace the two courses. Rani's last name, Humayun, recalls the Moghul emperor who spent most of his reign in exile.

Rani's name changes to Harappa and she is immured alive in a baroque mansion in Mohenjo's unending arid landscape that is 'afflicted by chronic water shortage, populated by scornful monsters' (*S*, 94). Mohenjo, Daro and Harappa combine to recall the ancient civilizations of the past. Instead of focusing on the advanced aspects of these cultures that flourished when the rest of the world was populated by primitive barbarians, Rushdie uses the setting as symbolic of stagnation and obsolescence. Negative traditionalism has Rani in throe here; she is surrounded by peasant girls who help themselves to her trousseau and ancient servants, 'in this house it's still what Isky's ayah says' (*S*. 93-94); her home is raided by barbarians who see women as possessions; occasionally, when Isky feels guilty about the isolation he has forced on her, he descends with an entourage of pimps and floozies, as Naveed would say, and upsets her further. Here everything is ruled by *takallouf,* a form of tongue-tying formality, a social restraint so extreme as to make it impossible for the victim to express what he or she really means, a species of compulsory irony that insists, for the sake of good form, on being taken literally (*S*, 104), as Rushdie defines it in the context of Bilquis and Raza.

Both women are victimized by tradition. But it is paradoxical, perhaps more ironical than paradoxical, that both find a measure of freedom because of tradition. Tradition dictates that a man should support his family no matter what; tradition dictates that a woman run her household no matter what. Despite the erosion of love and trust, the accretion of veneers in time gives a measure of solidity and stability. Money, the earning and saving of wealth, keeping accounts, and all the paraphernalia that goes with the amassing and spending of money, is never mentioned; that too is *takallouf.* Old Shakil would have died in debtors' prison in Dickens, and Bilquis and Rani spent years in law courts over maintenance and alimony in modern day Eurocentric soap operas and real life, but in the cultural setting of *Shame,* mentioning money or lack thereof is tabooed. Bilquis and Rani can and do have a material sense of security that is part of the package of this cultural misogyny. A man's home is his castle, the saying goes in one part of the world; in another part, a woman's home is her castle, even if it turns out to be a living tomb. Because of this, women can build a strange and sad kind of autonomy for themselves as we see with Bilquis, and especially with Rani.

But one trait that is absent in Bilquis and Rani is maternal love. Indeed, positive parental emotions are conspicuously absent in Rushdie's fiction. Whereas fathers are usually unforgiving and unforgivable in their dealings with their offspring, mothers have a cavalier spirit of abandonment towards their children. The mothers in his novels are not particularly maternal; none of them seems to have the character traits usually associated with mothers-gentleness, self-sacrifice, nurturance – all that can be said in their favour is that they do not inspire or instigate violence and abuse in their offspring the way fathers do. The mothers are indifferent, callous, or selfish. It is implied that Bilquis might have smacked or thrown Sufiya and brought about her retardation; the chasm between Rani and her daughter is wide enough to hold the Grand Canyon; Naveed has twenty-seven children but she is not a mother. The only one who is deeply desirous of having babies and loves them is Sufiya Zinobia. She plays with Naveed's babies as often she can. "She likes watching them crawl, fall over, make funny noises, likes knowing more than them. She skips for them: O the wonder in their eyes. (S, 214)"

Rushdie's handling of retarded children is sensitive and immensely poignant, as I have argued in my 'Girl Children in Rushdie's Novels'. (ed. by Viney Kirpal, 1991). It is significant that he makes them girls. Through his women, and girl children, Rushdie covers a wide range of injustices. He sums up his view of the effect of these injustices in two authorial appearances-the key passage about the three characters who inspired the character of Sufiya Zinobia (*S*, 115-17) and where he talks of women having taken over his narrative, which ends with:

> If you hold down one thing you hold down the adjoining. In the end, though, it all blows up in your face. (*S*, 173)

A family that ill treats its women will destroy itself, as happens at the end of the novel.

But what of the other women in *Shame*? Farah Zoroaster, Pinkie Aurangzeb, Arjumand Harappa and Naveed Hyder, strong characters every one of them, who march out and grabs father time/opportunity by the beard and drags him to her lair?

These characters' lives show they are a new breed of women, intelligent, astute, ambitious. Common to all is a braggadocio way of talking, a supreme confidence in oneself, an all out thrust at ignoring tradition in their search for self-fulfilment. All of them start or end with an uninhibited scorn for the opposite sex and the state of marriage.

Of the four, Arjumand is the only one who is trained for a profession other than housekeeping. Like the other women, her ambition is to be linked to a great man, to be the force behind his greatness. The man is her father, rather than the suitor fantasized by virginal Rani or the flesh and blood husband loved by bridal Bilquis. In words that echo Bilquis', Arjumand tells Isky, "What things won't you do? just wait and see" (*S*, 126). And when she echoes her mother's long-ago words about Omar Shakil, her father smiles in agreement. And when he tells her, "It's a man's world, Arjumand. Rise above your gender as you grow. This is no place to be a woman in (*S*, 126), she takes him at his word and thenceforward rejects her gender.

As she grows into womanhood, she spurns her body and makes herself look and behave like a man, flatchested and stern; she spurns men and when the crowd of suitors at the gate creates a perpetual traffic jam, she goes off to a women's college; but women fall in love with her as passionately and hopelessly as the men had, and she returns to her father, eager to be by his side as he rose to power. Then, Oedipus more than biology takes over; she falls in love with Haroun Harappa who looks exactly like her father did in youth. But Haroun's marriage is arranged with Naveed, and she retreats in rage, to be Virgin Ironpants then on. She is devastating as a lawyer. As a modernist, she reprimands her father for comparing his job of making 'this country as a man would build a marriage. With strength as well as caring'. She retorts, 'Polygamist . . . what an old-fashioned backward type at heart! It's just marriages and concubines you want. Modern man, my foot' (*S.* 183). But her father can do no wrong, and her world-view is that of a man, anyway. Women have no place in her life, not even her mother, Rani, whom she rejects because Rani refuses to go along with the Alexandrine myth that she builds around Isky.

In conclusion, Arjumand is a modernist who prepares herself to lead the country into progressive changes but she offers no model for the modern woman who feels it is her right to have both marriage and career. Arjumand is a prototype of the phase in Western feminism where women professionals paid the price of spinsterhood and/or childlessness. Moreover, her philosophy is too deeply imbued with the abrogation of human feelings and failings to be considered admirable. Most important, strong and independent though she is, she is too much a worshipper of a male hero to be an ideal new woman.

Farah Zoroaster is kindred spirit to foul-mouthed, brash Evie Lilith Burns of *Midnight's Children* and Azra who scorns the love of the postman early in *Shame.* Farah rides roughshod over Omar's amorous advances; her vocabulary and actions show not only her independence from traditional constraints but a conscious will to shock: "I shit on your words . . . you got the hots, no more to it than that" (*S,* 29). "Drop this jungle-boy business, you're no fucking apeman, sonny jim" (*S* 31). Like Evie, she kindles a passion that turns destructive when frustrated.

Saleem Sinai, the voyeur, gets into Evie's head; Omar Shakil, also a voyeur, takes the more common route of rape. Rushdie has Omar repeat his rationalization, "She was willing . . . she must have been willing, and everybody knows the risk" (*S*. 52) but in the slight variation, Rushdie encapsulates what psychiatrists and social workers have established as a clear pattern of self-exoneration in rapists and wife beaters: an illogical assumption that 'she *must have been* willing'. Rushdie excels in building up the reader's awareness of injustices meted out to women even while dealing with a quite unlikeable person.

Naveed is another such example. She alienates the reader from the moment she appears on stage as a pre-teenager. But looking deeper, the influence of traditional role-expectations is clear. Even at age ten, she is obsessed with the idea of getting married and wants long hair because she has heard that "men grow crazy for shiny hair that you can put under your bums" (*S*, 136). It should be noted that her obsession is for marriage and not directed towards promiscuity. When Bilquis brings forward the name of Haroun Harappa as a possible match, Naveed is brutally pragmatic: "I don't need to look at any stupid photograph," she told *Bilquis* "he's famous, he's rich, he's a husband, let's catch him quick." (*S*, 155)

In her supreme self-confidence, she says she'll 'fix him' when Bilquis points out that Haroun is 'bad to his daddy'. She flouts tradition and throws family honour to the winds when she backs out of the betrothal with a characteristic, 'I won't marry that stupid potato'. Love, as Rushdie says, 'was the last thing anyone had been expecting to foul up arrangements' (S, 165). In a traditional set-up one married for fame, riches, political advancement, not for love. Naveed struck out for love, for modernity in making matrimonial relationship. And what happened? Her husband came to her once a year and ordered her to get ready, because it was time to plant the seed, until she felt like a vegetable patch . . . and understood that there was no hope for women in the world, because whether you were respectable or not the men got you anyway, no matter how hard you tried to be the most proper of ladies the men would come and stuff you full of alien unwanted life. (*S*, 207)

Again, in a single sentence Rushdie summarizes the oppressive lot of women through a character who is quite unlikeable and yet who is so clearly a victim of a male-centred society that the reader is moved to sympathy. Naveed's fertility is symbolic of Pakistan's population explosion at the level of political allegory, but at the level of social satire, it only slightly exaggerates women's lack of autonomy in deciding when or when not to have children.

Pinkie Aurangzeb's position *vis-a-vis* tradition/modernity is more complex. She is yet another strong, self-confident woman. She has scant regard for the sanctity of marriage vows. She is Isky's twin soul in many ways. She flirts outrageously and picks up whomever she wants whenever she wants, But unlike Isky and Raza who have attractive helpmeets, Pinkie has a doddering old husband who knows how to hold his drink without spilling a drop even when asleep but is clearly good for little else. 'Trapped in a marriage with a dotard, Pinkie finds her pleasures wherever she can'. (*S*, 104) There is a hint of justification for her promiscuity.

Pinkie's is a complex case. Liaisons such as hers dot the pages of history, sometimes glamourized, sometimes held up an example of what not to be. So, one cannot rush to a hasty conclusion that she was being modernist in her unfaithfulness that modernist Rushdie seems to excuse, or that Rushdie has transplanted the salons of Paris to this locale. The pertinent question is, how does it all end? Thrown out unceremoniously by Isky, she remained faithful to him until the day of his death, when after setting fire to an old embroidered shawl, she hacked out her own heart with a nine-inch kitchen knife' (*S*,106).

It is difficult to surmise why Rushdie gave her this ending. Was it dictated by some real life analogy to the figures represented by Isky and Pinkie? Rushdie has obviously taken liberties with historical analogs in numerous instances in order to remain true to his muse; so why not now? or is this what his muse would endorse? Was it to redeem Pinkie's promiscuous image in the minds of traditionalists? Unlikely, given Rushdie's irreverent swipes at traditionalism. Was it to raise these lovers to some sort of Antony and Cleopatra level? Not likely, given his open dislike of Harappa and historical Bhutto.

Why then does he pack Pinkie off to the hereafter in this extremely traditional manner?

Pinkie Aurangzeb is the only woman in the novel who claims equality in terms of sexual freedom, doing what men traditionally do, namely, use the opposite sex for sexual gratification without any qualms of conscience. Farah is raped; Bilquis is seduced by a lewd-mouthed playboy. But Pinkie is her own woman, she picks and chooses, who excels in the game that is traditionally a male prerogative. Granted that two wrongs do not make a right and that the way to combat men's promiscuity is not by admiring or condoning the same behaviour in women; still, Pinkie's independence and initiative in sexual indulgence does arouse a streak of appreciation, and one feels regret that she turns out after all like the hundreds of heroines on the traditional Indian movie screen. Especially when taken in the context of the parade of women just analyzed, one wonders why Rushdie did not hold at least one example of an independent, strong-minded woman who approached sexual freedom with the same irreverent vitality that so many of his male characters assume. It is not indoctrinated traditionalism that restrained them for they were rebels as we have seen. It is not any saccharine sweetness of innate womanhood for most of them lack stereotypical womanly virtues and are quite unlikable. It is Rushdie, in short, and not the characters themselves who shape this aspect of their fate.

Yes, one wonders with deep dismay why all these women who deviate from the traditional role of faithful wife and devoted child-bearer come to grief. It is small comfort to be told, in the mode of Professor Higgins' rejoinder when Eliza contrasted his rudeness to Pickering's politeness, that even women who do not deviate from traditional role expectations come to grief in Rushdie. Rushdie, as one sensitive enough to know that the chains that bind women are no fictions, as one courageous, or imprudent, enough to challenge long established beliefs, could have given us a truly modernist woman.

Perhaps it could not be Arjumand because the political allegory did not quite permit it, but it could have been Farah who could have come back to Q. to be other than the old crone he makes her, or Rani who could have come into her own after Isky's death, or Pinkie Aurangzeb. Making Pinkie another of the thousand 'good bad-girl', to use Fiedler's classification for the Marilyn Monroe prototype, who could have died tear-jerker deaths on the silver screen of India is a lapse that is indeed regrettable.

## Works Cited

Atwood, Margaret. *Survival: A Thematic Guide to Canadian Literature.* Toronto: Anansi. 1972.

Daly, Mary. *Gyn/Ecology: The Meta Ethics of Radical Feminism*. Boston: Beacon. 1978.

Fiedler, Leslie. *Love and Death in the American Novel.* New York: Criterion Books. 1960.

Graves, Robert. *The White Goddess.* New York: American Book Stratford. 1948.

De Man, Paul. 'Nietzsche's Theory of Rhetoric,' *Symposium* 28 (1974).

Raja Rao. *The Serpent and the Rope,* London: John Murray, 1960.

Rushdie. Salman. *Grimus,* London: victor Gollacz, 1975.

— *Midnight s Children,* London: Jonathan Cape, 1981.

— *The Satanic Verses,* London: Penguin, 1988.

— *Shame,* London: Jonathan Cape, 1983 (identified as *S*).

# 11

# Girl Children in Rushdie's Fiction

In the light of contemporary critical theories, especially those that interconnect psychological analysis, sociological realism, structuralism and deconstructionism, one needs to re-read every novel from various perspectives. Edward Said's *Orientalism (1978)* and *The World, the Text and the Critic (1983)* have enunciated what many post-colonial readers and critics have felt about the western Judaeo-Christian-conditioned reading of Commonwealth Literature that often distorts the sensibility underlying a literary work. By endowing the imperialist self to have "a flexible positional superiority" the westerner can have a "whole series of relationships with the Orient without ever losing him the upper hand." For one who comes from the feminist perspective, warning lights start blinking whenever women are being delineated in fiction, and post-modernism and deconstructionism only hinder appreciation. The text is grounded in history and experience. Thirdly, from the perspective of intertextuality, the meanings which a work yields depends greatly on what the reader brings to it. The

---

This essay appeared as Chapter 28 in *The Girl Child in 20th Century Indian Literature*. Ed. Viney Kirpal. New Delhi: Sterling Publishers. 1992. pp. 267-278.

interpretation that one gives to Rushdie's delineation of girl children could vary widely; but starting with the above, I would like to explore another facet, namely, the influence of what Said calls "instinctual filiation" in *Beginnings, Intention and Method* (1975). He posits "instinctual filiation" as originating in nature, and "social affiliation" as associated with culture: Is "filiation" primordial? Was there a beginning that we can call natural filiation or is it so far back in the irretrievable and unimaginable past that it is lost and therefore irrelevant? Or is it waiting to be re-discovered? Do writers consciously or serendipitously, cerebrally or instinctually, create case histories that echo in their subtexts something quintessential about human motivations and actions?

In one's search for commonalities, one runs the risk of Procrustean criticism, stretching and selecting readings to fit one's hypotheses. Since all critics are Procrustean to varying degrees, having stated that caveat, I would say that the delineation of girl children in Indo-English literature is related to perceptions and reactions that come out of a pan-Indian ethos that is to be seen without the distortions of Orientalism, and is also related to the retrieving of the Other so that a connection is made with primordial filiation.

Perhaps it is a human and global tendency to look on children as Wordsworth did, that they come "trailing clouds of glory . . . from God who is our home"; it is also well recognised that trailing clouds of divinity notwithstanding, some children bring serious problems to adults and often feel unwanted. However the cultural component in different literatures adds a dimension of distinctness to universal elements. Indo-English writers tend to romanticise female children in a particular way. Hindu culture plays a major role in the pan-Indian ethos. The divinity of children, personified in the Krishna archetype, is ingrained in the Hindu sensibility. This, coupled with the concept of Shakti, the Mother Principle, makes the symbolisation of female children in literature take on an aura of mystique and mysticism. The paean of praise sung by Raja Rao's Rama to adolescent Saroja in *The Serpent and the Rope* and by Sivarama Sastri in *The Chessmaster and his Moves* might seem extravagant but they strike a chord in the Hindu reader:

> The woman is the miracle. She subsumes you with her presence, and makes you know yourself. *(The Chessmaster)*
>
> The pyramid I had seen, the one at Gizeh, would also be a temple, and Jayalakshmi my queen, my sister. (*The Chessmaster,* 102)
>
> Jaya's silences were like journeys into the interior, the pilgrimage to her occult sanctuary. She came out of it always carrying, as I have said before, the hieratic fruits and flowers and steps of worship. (*The Chessmaster,* 572)

On the other hand, sociologists and their ilk pounce on this view as a travesty of their perception of reality where female children are oppressed and starved in favour of their male siblings, and Eurocentric psychoanalysts see everything through sex-tinted glasses. One can hold a view that is at least as valid as theirs, namely that many Indian writers (in English and in regional languages) communicate the primordial sense of worship that inspired primitive man to perceive as female the primal creative force behind the manifested world. This sense persists even today in the pan-Indian ethos because Hinduism is one of the few religions that survived the near-global takeover of an androcentric power structure, and all regional and religious cultures in India have been influenced by it to leave room for the vital connection with the primordial. The concept of the Triple Goddess, as Mary Daly and others have discussed, was present in all ancient cultures, but was displaced in each by patriarchy. Daly summarizes the identity of the Triple Goddess in various ancient religions: Hera-Demeter-Kore of pre-Hellenic times, Thetis, Amphitrite, Nereis of Hellenic mythology, Neith Triple Goddess of Libya, Eire, Phodla, Banbha of Ireland, and Myrine who was mother of the gods in Phrygian lore. Daly relies unduly on Katherine Mayo's *Mother India (1927)* and the protests published in its wake, and so has not realised that among living religions, Hinduism alone survived the total takeover, and female manifestations-the Parvati-Lakshmi-Saraswathy triad are part, and often the major part of human perception of divinity.

Of the many theorists who have dealt with the concept of the Other, Simone de Beauvoir's exposition of how it affects gender relations is a good starting point since her feminism and

Said's views on Orientalism converge in the present context. Critics of Commonwealth literature have followed the concept of the Other to explain imperialist power structures that have subjugated cultural identity in countries once ruled by the British. Feminists have explained how masculinist traditions have reinforced and perpetuated the habit of seeing the subject as always male, and have pushed women into "objecthood" so that even women see themselves and other women as objects. The Other is usually seen as object-inferior, controllable and invariably controlled.

Feminism seeks to retrieve the sense of self, of' female as subject, of women as controllers rather than the controlled. In this paradigm, writers portray characters who instinctively or consciously shrug off the traditional role and expectations of their gender, and control their personal space. This is done either by dominating others or by distancing themselves from others so as to become invulnerable to external threats of depredation. What I am seeking, in short, is to redefine the Other along the lines of Rushdie's phrase, "The Empire Strikes Back." He uses it in the context of how the periphery has now become the centre in that the best literature today is coming from the peripheries of the erstwhile Raj. Similarly, it is my contention that the Other is striking back by measuring the rest in terms of itself and thus placing itself in control. Indo-English writers often see women as the Other but as a somewhat exalted Other rather than as the subjugated Other. This is very different from the patriarchal view as also from the archetype of "woman on a pedestal" which is yet another form of oppression. In Rushdie's world, women are the redefined Other, in control of their personal space and sometimes of others as well. Rushdie incorporates the exalted Other without in any way ignoring the oppression and suppression imposed on women. His women suffer but arouse more admiration than mere pity.

Rushdie handles girl children very differently from other Indo-English writers. Like him, other writers recognise that children have a way of creating their own personal space, but they tend to adulate their child characters. Starting from Henry Louis Derozio's "Fakeer of Jungheera" and Romesh Chandra Dutt's Christianized retelling of the *Mahabharata,* one comes to familiar examples in the works of the giants of the present century: Tagore's "Kabuliwallah," Sri Aurobindo's delineation of child Savitri, and R.K. Narayan's Leela in *The English Teacher.* Narayan might be taken as representative of this group.

In R.K. Narayan's earliest stories and novels we find a deftness and insight in the handling of children and the child world that is missing in his later work. In his later novels, children are merely secondary characters who highlight the idiosyncrasy or attitudes of adults; the point of view is always the adult's; the author seldom gets into the child's identity, and on the rare occasions he does, he fails to carry the reader along with him.

In one of the stories in his *Lawley Road,* "The Birthday Gift," the rivalry between Seenu and his sister Seetha provides much of the humour. Rather than continue to be blackmailed by Seetha, Seenu confesses to his father that he has lost his treasured pen, and finds he can once again defend himself against her demands and trickery.

However, except for Seetha, whom he makes realistically sweet and manipulative by turn, Narayan has so soft a corner in his heart for little girls that he overly romanticises most of them. But they too are delightful delineations. Shanta, in "Forty Five a Month" is a predecessor to Leela in *The English Teacher.* Her father has promised to take her to the cinema, and she is wildly excited. The reader can readily feel her throbbing impatience coming through the printed words as she keeps asking from two o'clock onwards if it is five o'clock. Too excited even to eat, she has her mother deck her out in her favourite clothes and trips time and again to the end of the road and back, waiting for her father. But her father, kept overtime by his inconsiderate employer, returns home only at nine o'clock-to see that the child has fallen asleep in her pink dress.

Leela in *The English Teacher* is a lovely portrait of a three-year old girl. The whole novel is written in a higher key than the others, being the most autobiographical of his works and especially poignant because of the early death of Krishnan's (Narayan's) wife. After Susila's death, Krishnan's life settles to a new routine. Leela is always up and by her father's bedside before he awakes; in the evening, he reads to her, but insists that she have a wash before they settle down to read.

> "Why?"
>
> "That is how it must be done."
>
> "No. We must first read stories," she corrected me.
>
> "We must first wash, and then read stories," I persisted.
>
> "Why?"
>
> "Because it is Goddess Saraswathi and we must never touch her without washing."
>
> "What will she do if we touch her without washing?"
>
> "She will be very unhappy, and she is the Goddess of Learning, you see, and if you please her by washing and being clean, she will make you very learned."
>
> "Why should I be learned?"
>
> "So you can read a lot of stones yourself without my help."
>
> "Oh, what will you do then?" she asked, as if pitying a man who would lose his only employment in life." *(The English Teacher, 115-16).*

The exchanges between father and daughter are commonplace enough, and yet they give an average Indian reader what Sean O'Faolain calls the pleasure of recognition that gives unfailing satisfaction. As with so much of Narayan's gentle sermonising, this exchange educates the non-Indian reader into one of the essential traits of the Hindu ethos, namely, respect for learning and for books, that is ingrained into the child mind by parents and teachers.

In Narayan's fiction children, especially girl children, are the exalted Other, physically in the control of adults but emotionally controlling them.

When we come to Rushdie, are we on a different planet altogether? With his customary irreverent abandon, Rushdie rushes headlong into demythicising everything and everyone.

His women deserve a longer analysis than is relevant here. All his women are far more extreme in their response to the world than the males around them. In my study (under preparation) of Rushdie's feminism, my central hypothesis is that despite his debunking of the "gentler sex" myth, Rushdie in essence takes a romantic view of female symbolisation; he endows many of his females with far more power, more mystique and more survival capabilities than possessed by his male characters. At the same time he is fully aware of how they have been exploited, and his delineation of Sufiya Zinobia in *Shame* reveals a compassion that does not usually come to the surface in his writing. We see Rushdie's pro-feminist sensibility in some of the essays of his latest volume, *Imaginary Homelands.* He ends his review of Anita Desai, *In Custody* saying that in having Deven commit himself to the aging poet and ignoring both his wife and Nur's, Desai has shown the irony of women's lives. "That Anita Desai has so brilliantly portrayed the world of male friendship in order to demonstrate how this, too, is part of the process by which women are excluded from power over their own lives is a bitter irony behind what is an anguished, but not at all a bitter book." (73)

What Rushdie says half-facetiously in *Shame is* true of all his novels: Women have taken over. Rushdie's women are powerful forces; naturally enough, his girls are spirited creatures in control of their own world despite their traditional environment and the seemingly fight control of the adults.

There are not too many girl children in Rushdie's fictional world *(Grimus* and *The Satanic Verses* do not have any major child characters, though Ayesha in the latter could be seen as a child figure) but those that do appear in *Midnight's Children's* and *Shame* are vibrant characters.

In *Midnight's Children,* we have three girls in all – Evie, Jamila and Toxy Catrack. Two of them can be called rebels, tomboys, regular brats, indeed anything but the more common appellations signifying traditional female traits of gentleness, passivity, docility, physical weakness etc. They are Evie, who is an integral phase of Saleem Sinai's initiation into adulthood, and his sister Brass Monkey who grows up to be Jamila Singer, the person behind Pakistan's most popular and patriotic radio voice.

Through them, we see facets of Saleem's growing personality, but each is a distinct characterisation, even though Evie's part is a transient one.

Evie comes into Saleem's life for six months when he is ten years old and she ten and a half. As with his other names, Shiva, Parvati and Padma, with characteristic bluntness Rushdie gives her a middle name that goes beyond a name into archetype: Lilith. In Hebrew folklore, Lilith was Adam's first wife; in Babylonian folklore she was a female demon who inhabited ruins; and in medieval folklore, she was a witch; in the six months she spends in Bombay before returning to the United States, Evie proves herself aptly named.

Evie makes a dramatic appearance on New Year's Day, 1957. When Saleem and other boys of Methwold's Estate are playing French cricket, she charges in on her two-wheeler and performs a circus act that leaves them openmouthed. She does breathtaking feats on the bike: headstand, reverse pedalling, and shooting at moving targets with a Daisy air-pistol. Saleem, whom she greets with a "Hey, you widda leaky nose!" falls in love with her instantly. Evie is a power among them, no question.

Evie is definitely the Other in more ways than one. She is American, and can be seen as symbolic of the new Imperialism of the Coca Cola empire that so quickly and effectively has taken over most of the world with its fast foods, fizzy drinks, and foamy lifestyle, and that proliferates without centre or soul. It is to be noted that she, an American, takes over Methwold Estate that Methwold had thought he had frozen perpetually British in time. If one continues this metaphor where the British are replaced by Americans, is there prophecy in the unceremonious way she is scuttled out of the country?

One could carry the metaphor in a different direction. Evie is part of Saleem's initiation into adulthood; more importantly, she is the catalyst that brings him the second instalment of his inheritance as Midnight's first child, in that his headlong crash into the language demonstration crowd during his attempt to impress her with his painstakingly learned art of cycling makes him identify the voices in his head. But most importantly in the present context, her final act of shooting cats (for a bounty) with her Daisy pistol and the consequent act of Brass Monkey's brings about a feeling in Saleem that his sister did it for him. He says, "Evie and my sister (who were, in many ways, not at all dissimilar)" were fighting over him, and "the strength of the Monkey was the strength of sibling loyalty, and her act of war was actually an act of love" *(MNC* 226). It is interesting to note not only foreshadowing in the choice of phrase but the pattern of twin selves when referring to Evie and Monkey, a pattern that recurs in all of Rushdie's fiction – Grimus-Flapping Eagle, SaleemShiva, Isky-Raza, Farishta-Saladin. In having the Monkey establish supremacy over Evie, and Saleem vanquish Evie in his own way by entering her brain, Rushdie is aligning Evie with Grimus, Shiva and Farishta, the evil half of the recurring pattern of dichotomous selves.

Evie is "not dissimilar" to the Monkey; Saleem is in love with each, at different times; both are spirited and independent; both hold admirers in disdain, though Evie has a partiality for Sonny Ibrahim, and both seem totally self-contained, as are Ayesha and Sufiya elsewhere. (Incidentally, there is an intriguing similarity between Rushdie's cycle of incestuous linkages of characters and Raja Rao's in *The Chessmaster.)* The Brass Monkey's acts of violence are as destructive as Evie's-"count the windows and vases, broken accidentally-on-purpose; number if you can, the meals that somehow flew off her treacherous dinner-plates to stain valuable Persian rugs . . . the ruins of broken chairs and shattered ornaments" *(MNC* 151). She goes through various phases such as burning any pair of shoes she can find. *But she is only mischievous, whereas there is an unmistakably evil streak in Evie.* The Brass Monkey, with her propensity to talk to birds and animals, seems to have Said's "instinctual filiation."

One of the remarkable traits of Indian life and literature is the acceptance of abnormalities and disabilities. Village idiots, eunuchs, transsexuals, transvestites, all have a place; however rude the village boys might be, there always seem to be enough compassionate villagers to take care of the idiot's material needs. They are not shut away as in Victorian life or literature. Rushdie laughs at Zafar's enuresis but is extremely sensitive about the Monkey's disability of never reaching puberty, proving once again that girl children occupy a special place. He is also far more compassionate towards mentally handicapped girl children than towards retarded boy children as can be seen in his handling of Alexei Cherkassov in *Grimus* and of Toxy Catrack in *Midnight's Children* and Ayesha in *The Satanic Verses.*

Toxy Catrack is a forerunner of Sufiya Zirtobia. Toxy is a minor character and there is no intrasubjective discourse between her and the others, but in Sufiya's case, this discourse starts at birth and continues through life. The main interaction is between Sufiya and her parents. Whereas both react to her birth with unhidden disappointment because she is not male, in the latter part of her life, her father moves closer to her. In contrast, the mother first feels doubly guilty for not having a boy and for her inability to love Sufiya. Once Sufiya gets the bran fever that makes her an idiot, Bilquis keeps her distance and gives over her maternal role to the Parsi nurse, Shahbanou. There is a passage that leads to the inference that Bilquis did nurture the child.

> Once, when she picked up her damaged daughter to play the traditional game of water-carrier, swinging Sufiya Zinobia on her back and pretending she was a water-skin, she collapsed to the ground beneath the delighted child before she had finished pouring her out *(Shame 103).*

But Rushdie undercuts this with a later comment that perhaps it was not a fever that made her an idiot but her mother's blows. It is mentioned several times that Bilquis not only bombards her with abusive language but rains blows on her. Later, she is instrumental in miseducating her about marital sex by saying she should think of herself as a sea and her husband as a fish. Sufiya hates fish and the die is cast. The Beast in her rises when her husband inadvertently tells her to lie down. The battle between the Beauty and the Beast is an echo of the battle between Flapping Eagle and Grimus, between Saleem and Shiva, Farishta and Chamcha. Beauty wins, this time, and Shakil is saved.

The movement of reconciliation of Raza Hyder towards his retarded daughter comes about on the day she decapitates Pinkie Aurangzeb's more than two hundred turkeys. Sufiya obviously did it to please her mother who had been vociferously complaining about the turkey invasion, but her mother brutally punishes her. Her father however, views her with admiration despite his revulsion. After Bilquis cuts off the girl's hair, he picks her up "with a gentleness born of his infinite puzzlement and carries her indoors" *(Shame,* 140). From then on, he

> discovered that he could no longer see her through the veil of his disappointment in her sex. The memory of the tenderness with which he had lifted her out of the scene of her somnambulist violence refused to leave him . . . *(Shame, 160).*

Once Raza Hyder starts loving his child and spending time with her, her mental growth is accelerated. Rushdie's bias is apparent because here and elsewhere, there seems to be little love expressed between mothers and daughters; fathers and sons, whereas there is a strong bond between parents and their children of the sex opposite their own. Years later, she sustains herself with the happy memories she has hoarded from this period.

> Inside her head the precious fragile toys. One of the best things inside is when her father picks her up. Hugs, smiles at, cries over her. Says things she doesn't really understand, but the sounds are nice. She takes him out of her head and makes him do it over and over . . . . You can't do that with things outside your head.

But Sufiya, starving for maternal love, conjures up a favourite activity with her mother.

> her mother skips with her. Bilquis holds the skipping rope and two of them jump together, faster faster, until they are going so fast you cant see who is who any more, they could be one person within the circle of rope *(Shame 213).*

Her mother's rejection of her is in deep contrast to her father's love. But his love is put to the test and he fails. After Sufiya's decapitation of the four young men, he fears for his career and thinks of doing her in. He rationalises it as akin to Abraham's sacrifice.

Shakil refuses to accede to the plan. Is it love that motivates him or is it the Hippocratean oath of his profession or the professional challenge posed by his wife's illness?

Sufiya is different things to different characters around her and to different kinds of readers. Her relationship with her father is the most touching aspect of her experience and her positive influence. But she clearly stands for more than herself; she stands for all retarded children who are doubly abused by the system and the people around them; she stands-for all women who are victims of violence, as Rushdie explicates through the real life stories that inspired this character. She is the personification of shame, a Christ-like figure who takes on the shame of the shameless like a sponge and thus purifies the atmosphere.

In the metaphorical context, Sufiya is the embodiment of the country, Pakistan, which had hoped to live up to its name-Land of the Pure. A country that is a miracle gone wrong.

From one point of view Sufiya's hysteria may be seen as "an unconscious form of feminist protest" to use Elaine Showalter's words, or it can be seen as the desperate communication of the powerless because madness is "the impasse confronting those whom cultural conditioning has deprived of the very means of protest or self-affirmation" as Showalter cites from Shoshana Felman's *Women and Madness*. This reading could be developed further in light of Gilbert and Gubar's *Madwoman in the Attic*, an erudite analysis of nineteenth century women characters who are literally and figuratively hidden away.

From another point of view, Sufiya can be seen as a manifestation of an avenging goddess. Rushdie combines both views when he explains that Sufiya is made up of two real-life girls who had been victims of violence because of their gender, and how he wished they would retaliate and destroy their attackers. The concept of an avenging goddess can be understood only by those who have pierced the phalanx of Orientalism that even most feminists (regrettably) have built, and enter the pan-Indian ethos which is, after all, the primordial truth apprehended by pre-patriarchal humans. The destructiveness of Evie is different from the destructiveness of Brass Monkey and Sufiya in the same way that Surpanaka and the coterie of demon powers differ from Durga and all her manifestations of primeval Shakti.

In the final analysis Sufiya is a force that destroys what ought to be destroyed. Her final act of destruction is seen by Shakil as the act of his retarded patient who has been taken over by the Beast; but as in Grimus, it is the final act of dissolution of a corrupt world.

## Works Cited

Daly, Mary. *Gyn/Ecology*. Boston: Beacon Press. 1978.

Narayan, R.K. *Lawley Road*. Delhi: Orient Paperbacks (Stories originally published in *Dodu and Other Stories* 1943).

—.*The English Teacher*. Mysore: Indian Thought Publications. 1946.

Rao, Raja. *The Chessmaster and his Moves*. New Delhi: Vision Books, 1988.

Rushdie, Salman. *Shame*. London: Jonathan Cape. 1983.

—. *Imaginary Homelands*. London: Granta Books. 1991, p. 73.

—. *Grimus*. London: Crafton Books. 1977.

—. *The Satanic Verses*. New York: Viking. 1988.

—. *Midnight's Children. London: Picador* (Pan Books). 1981.

Said, Edward. *Orientalism*. London: Routledge and Kegan Paul. 1978.

—. *The World, the Text and the Critic*. Cambridge: Harvard University Press. 1983.

—. *Beginnings, Intention and Method*. New York: Basic Books. 1975.

Showalter, Elaine. *The Female Malady: Women, Madness and English Culture 1830-1980*. New York: Pantheon Books. 1955.

# 12

# Purdah in Salman Rushdie, Attia Hosain and Rama Mehta

A lesson that is quickly learned by anyone who is frequently called upon to speak on India is that nothing about India can be reduced to an either-or, true-or-false conclusion. Given India's geographical, historical, political and cultural diversity, everything anyone says about India is likely to be partially true and partially false. Any analysis of purdah, like that of dowry and dowry related deaths, child labour and infanticide, spousal abuse and oppression of women, must have the same caveat that no generalisations are possible about national or cultural attitudes pertaining to India. Thus, the concept of literature as a mirror of society, that is often used in the context of post-colonial writings, has to start with the same caveat. It is more practical to confine oneself to what specific novels or novelists seem to say about any specific topic.

---

This essay was published in *Margins of Erasure: Purdah in the Subcontinental Novel in English*. Eds. Jasbir Jain and Amina Amin. New Delhi: Sterling Publishers. 1995. pp. 33-48.

Studying the occurrence and delineation of purdah in Indo-English literature is not as controversial as the other topics but it too needs an understanding of historical cultural bases in addition to skills of literary analysis. The word "purdah" has two related but distinct meanings. One is physical, in the sense of women wearing a veil or burqa to cover their faces from public view; the other is more complex and attitudinal, in the sense of a social norm whereby women live in seclusion, both from men and from the sphere of civic and public action. Further, one might be in purdah, in both ways, and still be in control of individual and public affairs as attested by earlier literatures about the power wielded by the women behind veils and lattice screens. Similarly, one might not be in purdah and yet could be attitudinally influenced by purdah culture, and this is the aspect that most concerns writers and society now that burqas, ghunghats and zenanas are becoming obsolete.

Of the three novels selected here, Attia Hosain's *Sunlight on a Broken Column* and Rama Mehta's *Inside the Haveli* give an authentic glimpse of purdah at both levels of meaning but focus more on the physical veil and physical seclusion; Salman Rushdie's *Shame,* on the other hand, refers to the physical veil only in passing but comments profoundly on what happens to women and to society when women live separated from men and public affairs. Attia Hosain's novel is set in the 1940s, when educated Muslim women were born in a zenana environment but grew up in an age of change. Rama Mehta's novel gives an intimate look at the day-to-day routine in a Hindu purdah family in Udaipur in the early 1950s; Rushdie's novel does not deal with zenanas and purdah at the literal level of veils, but comments on how the psyche of a purdah based culture ("purdah mentality" as Shahida Lateef calls it in *Muslim Women in India)* affected all of Pakistani society and politics. As with the perforated sheet in *Midnight's Children,* the purdah becomes profoundly symbolic in *Shame.*

Historically, it appears that purdah, in the sense of wearing a veil that hides a woman's face, was introduced into Indian society only after the advent of the Muslims (Altetkar, 1962). Ancient texts make no mention of purdah in this sense, though they show that women had their own quarters, the anthapuram, which was their private domain. The hymns of RgVeda X, for example, say clearly that women, whether bride or elder, should appear and speak to others with composure. Classical drama and dramaturgy bear evidence to the conclusion that women's costumes and access to public appearance were comparable to men's. The sculptures of Sanchi (2nd century B.C.) show that women did not wear veils, as do the frescoes of Ajanta and Ellora (A.D. 600-800) Early travellers, such as Yuan Chuang (A.D. 7th cent.) and Abu Zaid (A.D. 10th cent.) do not record anything about purdah. Women, at all times and in most regions, were more restricted in their mobility than men, but veils as such are rarely mentioned until the Muslim arrival in India. Altetkar shows that only women in the upper echelons were said to wear ornamental veils during pre-Muslim eras (Chapter 6). All the above also show that highborn men wore almost as much jewellery as highborn women, and that in paintings, sculptures and literature women were often set amidst public scenes such as the marketplace.

The initial reason why Hindu women took to purdah after the advent of Muslims is understandable: in order to protect themselves from the looks and actions of these invading strangers, women hid their faces behind veils and stayed in zenanas, or were made to do so by their men-folk. But then something peculiar and ironic happened. Mehta's novel repeats this several times. Because purdah was part of the Muslim court tradition and Muslims were rapidly extending their suzerainty, it was seen as a symbol of "having arrived", and Hindus adopted the custom as they moved upward on the social ladder! The modern analogy is the popularisation of bottle-feeding of babies instead of breastfeeding, or using white sugar and white rice and white flour instead of jaggery, parboiled rice and stone-ground flour. But the tide inevitably turns; just as avant garde "elites" in North America are going back to nature in their dietary habits, the elite of the early decades of this century moved back to reassert the old values of freedom and identity through "progress". All three novels deal with the evolution of this progress.

Each of the three novelists essentially says that purdah is a social custom that has outlived its day, but together these novels offer an interesting insight on how each author introduces his/her own perspective. Rushdie's Aadam Aziz directly orders his wife Naseern; in *Midnight's Children,* to come out of burqa and this leads to her coming out of purdah in the larger sense; because of a man's initiative a woman grows into her full potential. Mehta's Geeta, Bombay educated and ignorant of Purdah culture, learns to accept and even appreciate its values but initiates a slow transition among others through education; a woman's love for her husband makes her realise the securities of a collective system which allows for change and progress when an educated woman handles it the right way. Hosain's Laila quietly moves out of the zenana and into the arms of love; she gets this strength because her father's wishes and aunt's efforts have educated her to become an individual who can absorb the best from the world around her. Of the three, Hosain's novel is the most artistic in terms of melding social commentary into the narrative. Rushdie and Mehta use the story to make a point, and both use purdah as a metaphor for a more significant point; Hosain makes the point while telling the story. Hosain's novel is the most successful in the present context because there is such a fine balance in her craft at every step, between men and women, between tradition and change, between reason and emotion. Rushdie's *Shame,* however, moves at a very different level of art and metaphor. As with all his novels, its underpinnings of social and political commentary take the form of exaggeration and satirical humour.

The custom of purdah lends itself to both excessive romanticism and irate criticism. It has both an aura of idealisation and adverse implications of oppression of women; perpetuation of subservience and patriarchal power hierarchies. The latter view predominates in contemporary post-colonial and feminist critical discourses; given the commonalities of power paradigms that form the locus of critical analysis, it is both feasible and facile to use the same terms in both discourses: colonist/colonised, oppressor/oppressed, centre/periphery, dominant/other. Edward Said's *Orientalism,* one of the most quoted texts today, gives the core metaphor that brings the two discourses together that the Orientalist in seeing the colonist/colonised relationship in sexual terms reduces the colonised cultures to a female mystery that has to be mastered through violent penetration. Gayatri Chakravorty Spivak and her associates in the *Subaltern Studies Collective* have effectively unpacked the romanticism that was part of the Orientalist baggage and shown it as moth-eaten fake furs worthy only of being discarded wholesale. Isak Dinesen's short story, "The Blank Page", which has been made into a core metaphor for feminist texts by Susan Gubar's ammunition filled essay, "The Blank Page" and the "Issues of Female Creativity" (Showalter, 292-313), further extends the sociopolitical and literary parallels between post-colonial and feminist discourses.

But is there yet another way of reading these texts? One or more subversive ways that go beyond the middle road between the romanticists and the iconoclasts?

Take, for example, "The Blank Page"; it is a story of – a Carmelite Convent in Portugal where the nuns have for generations spun bridal sheets for princesses out of the finest cotton grown in their fields. After the ritual flag-waving of the sheet stained with hymenal blood on the day following the bridal night, the sheet is taken back to the convent, and the blood-stained spot framed and displayed in a hall; among all the framed sheets, there is one that is lily white, and women of all ages who come to this pilgrimage shrine stop for a long time in front of this. "When the storyteller is loyal, eternally and unswervingly loyal to the story, there, in the end, silence will speak," the old storyteller says before she tells the story of the blank page. Gubar's brilliant essay makes the blank page a metaphor for male writers' delineation of women and for women's writing, for both the possessive penetration and takeover of women-characters by male authors and the resistance and persistence of the women writers, who tell their stories through silence.

Ambiguity is the principal strategy in the story. The reason for the blank could be one of at least two alternatives: that the bride was not a virgin and by implication a rebel, or that she resisted and so was a rebel. The story is an example of the esoteric route of women's writings where while stating the oppressive display of male power over females, it also reveals the power of resistance and/or rebellion. Could there not be a third alternative, namely, that the groom was impotent? Thus the story could be seen as opening up a deeper subversive level of a possible pre-patriarchal society where the ritual of the bridal sheet could have been a test for the bridegroom's virility rather than for the bride's virginity. Would the groom who could not prove his virility by waving a crimson flag from the ramparts of the castle have been thrown down from the same ramparts if he failed? While this mythical recreation of another phase of societal evolution might be verging on wishful thinking, it might also be verging on mythopoeic truth. Western psychology's adumbration of masculine fears of castration and impotence are rooted in the gender-rooted apprehensions of an earlier time when men instinctively or otherwise accepted a feminised view of creation and power. It is standard political strategy for a usurper to try to destroy the roots of the empire he takes over (the Turks' policy of burning libraries when taking over the Byzantine empire, for example) or incorporate it so that its identity is subsumed (Christian adaptation of pre-Christian seasonal festivals, for example).

Ashis Nandy argues somewhat along these lines in "Woman versus Womanliness" where he says the masculine takeover was never final, and that the average Indian male still sees the feminine as the stronger force and struggles in an ambivalence:

> At one plane, he is continually afraid that he may become too autonomous of the maternal principle of authority, too defiant as a son of the power of cosmic motherhood, and too close to open anger towards his mother. On the other, he is constantly anxious that he will be incorporated by an all encompassing, powerful mother, lose his autonomy and individuality altogether, and be reduced to the "safe" but totally ineffective role of the father (Nandy, 153).

This ambivalence is what causes both the oppression and romanticising. But the point I wish to make is that simply because a male dominated system oppresses and/or romanticises women, women's identities are not to be defined by them because that would be to limit oneself to the language and parameters of the masculine mode. Women are inherently the stronger sex and their strength, when suppressed, goes underground to surface at another time in another form. Rushdie's Sufiya Zenobia is an extreme example of negative surfacing while Mehta's Geeta and Hosain's Laila are examples of moderately positive surfacing.

One has to go farther than arguing that men and masculinist systems oppress/romanticise women or that women oppress/romanticise women; however, both these lines of argument are valid and can very easily be drawn through all three novels.

In *Inside the Haveli,* for instance, women seem to be women's worst oppressors; Geeta, new bride, is greeted at the railway station by a woman who pulled her (Geeta's) sari over her face, and exclaimed in horror, "Where do you come from that you show your face to the world?" Pari, the senior servant maid, who has almost as much authority as Geeta's mother-in-law, twice repeats the same injunction even before Geeta has stepped into the haveli: In the first sixteen pages, Mehta sets up the pervasiveness of purdah by having no less than nine references to the importance of covering one's face. It becomes a metaphor for Geeta's new life even as it authentically records a culture. But it is very clear that women stand by each other; Lakshmi's abandoned child, for example, becomes part of the haveli family, as a matter of course, and Pari becomes Geeta's chief mentor. While there is little doubt that the male dominated system confines women, it is also clear that the men are honourable and with a steadfast sense of duty. When Geeta looks at them from her balcony, "a glow of pride and affection filled Geeta . . . . Looking at the men below, she forgot her daily irritations" (Mehta, 35). It is Ajay's sense of duty and loyalty that makes him stay on in the haveli instead of leaving for Delhi. As M. S. Gore points out, males were also subject to the control of the patriarch and so could not support their wives' bid for autonomy and self-individuation even when they wished to (Gore, 1968, 150). But the separateness of the lives of men and women leads to different forms of oppression for both sexes.

Men and women oppress each other. Obversely, men and women romanticize each other and the culture in all three novels. Indeed, *Inside the Haveli is* simultaneously a sensitive description of life in purdah and a justification of it for the given time and place. It is an elegy for "the days when everything was bright and gay, when the Rana sat on his throne and received his people, rich and poor alike. No one in the city can forget those days when Udaipur belonged to the people" (Mehta, 2). The novel is an extension of Rama Mehta's sociological study of the Oswal community of Udaipur where she concludes that "tradition and modernity can be combined and are not necessarily antithetical to each other" (Nanda, 127). Its theme is that there was much beauty and honour in the old ways, and that as we move into our own times and place, we would do well to recognise the bond that exists between traditions and its insiders. Outsiders tend to dismiss the bond with facile cliches about the dependence prisoners develop towards their warders or victims towards their oppressors. A parallel text to Inside the Haveli is a work published in the 1940s: Hilda Wernher's My *Indian Family,* an autobiographical narrative. The narrator is a European woman who comes to India to be with her daughter Mary Ann who has married a Muslim, Rashid Ali. Mary Ann dies within a year in an accident; Hilda stays on to comfort Rashid, and in due time arranges another marriage for him. Just as Geeta, a Bombay progressive is gradually drawn to love the haveli, Hilda is gradually drawn into India. "The stranger, the Westerner, had been-adopted by Indian hearts" (Wernher, 13). Just as *Inside the Haveli* ends with Geeta assuming her role as they mistress of the haveli and its traditions, *My Indian Family* ends with, "I only know that this is India, and that I am thousands of miles away from my own people, and yet at home" (Wernher, 298). Both Hilda and Mary Ann feel strongly about white women who come to India to marry an Indian without loving India. "It is not enough to love the man; one must love India as well" (92); "A European girl coming out, knowing and caring nothing about India, only about the man she loves or thinks she loves" (231). But both novels show that loving a man could, at times, lead a woman to love his traditional purdah culture.

Looked at one way all three novelists, Hosain, Mehta and Rushdie, give expression to the romantic view. Aadam Aziz's first reaction to seeing his purdahed patient has the same romantic passion as the more traditional scenes of Hindi movies where the "hero" gets a glimpse of the "heroine's" hand or braid. Who can forget the passion and ecstasy of that movie of another age, 'Chaudhvin Ka Chand', as Waheeda Rehman's veil is lifted and Guru Dutt sees her wondrous beauty? Who does not recognise with a thrill-the foreshadowing in the scene where Laila, being teased by Zahra about some hypothetical bridegroom whose face she would see in the nuptial mirror, sees Asad's reflection as he barges in for a moment? (Hosain, 148). Who cannot instinctively empathise with Geeta when she says she came to love the veil that hid her face because it allowed her to think while others talked, allowed her to see everything without being seen? (Mehta, 19). It is easy enough to dismiss these as highly idealised and unreal moments that ignore the sordidness of systemic exploitation, and yet . . . .

There is a difference between sentiment and the sentimental, between romanticism and romanticised love. We need sentiment and romance while the sentimental and romanticised must go out the window. But what if they cannot be separated without some irreparable loss? Aadam Aziz's first mission after getting married is to get Naseem to shed purdah. Naseem grows to become Reverend Mother, an extremely efficient housekeeper and matriarch, but the magic of romantic passion is gone. It is the same with Mumtaz. Her life with Nadir in the cellar is a literal metaphor for purdah. They are totally secluded and totally protected. It is an unnatural way of life because purdah is only for women and Nadir Khan, by living in purdah; becomes womanised, impotent. However, Mumtaz would rather have the romanticism of a poetic and impotent lover than the dullness of a prosaic and virile husband, the magnificent marble tomb of her royal namesake than the workaday proliferation of; a workaday woman. Eros and Thanatos take on another dimension. Divorced from Nadir, Mumtaz descends to a more mundane life as wife and mother, as social and civic being.

At the literal level, however, Aadam Aziz, acting in the second decade of this century, is in the vanguard of the purdah abolition movement. It was only in the 1920s that the Women's Movement had gathered enough momentum under the leadership of the All India Women's Congress to make the removal of purdah one of is top priorities. As Manmohan Kaur records, when the Begum of Bhopal symbolically removed her veil during her presidential speech in 1929, it was a gesture that unequivocally stated that women were taking their own initiatives to come out of zenanas and educate themselves to participate in public life (Kaur, 26).

The perforated sheet is certainly a metaphor for one's quest for the meaning of life; we can never see the whole but can only look through bits and pieces disparately. To use Yeats's words play, "Nothing can be sole or whole that has not been rent" ("Crazy Jane"). But it is also a metaphor for the magic of life, to see life openly stretched out makes life lifeless, leaving no room for imagination, for idealisation. In our insistence on dissecting and laying bare everything, we kill the essence. An artist needs the mystery, the aura. Recognising that the best parts of our individual and collective selves are sustained by symbols rather than facts, and that symbols are after all rooted in latent reality, creative writers tend towards the romantic. All three, Rushdie, Mehta and Hosain, basically disapprove of the purdah and show how it has wrongfully restricted women's freedom and growth and yet all three view it with some nostalgia in that it brought some magic into life, both of women and men. Rather than seeing the women as survivors and the men as oppressors orb accessories to oppression, as many post-colonial and feminist readers might, relationships can be seen to embody the artistic tensions needed for continual evolution. The authors affirm that the romantic has a place but they do not justify purdah.

A contrast would exemplify my point. Neguib Mahfouz's *Palace Walk*, set in Cairo, provides this contrast through narrative strategies that are weighted, perhaps unintentionally, towards the priorities of purdah culture. Amina, married at fourteen, has never moved beyond the narrow confines of her house and routine, and never gone anywhere without her husband's knowledge and permission. In her forties, with five grown children, she yields to a lifelong temptation that is totally religious – "A visit to the shrine of al-Husayn is something my heart has wished for all my life . . . but . . . your father?" Her son assures her that his father, away in Port Said, would never know. "As an extra precaution you can borrow Umm Hanafi's wrap, so anyone who sees you leaving the house or returning will think you're a visitor" (Mahfouz, 165). "As she crossed the threshold of the outer door and entered the street, she experienced a moment of panic. Her mouth felt dry. She had an oppressive feeling of doing something wrong." Later, "with joy singing in her breast" she steps into the shrine and "she felt that her body was dissolving into tenderness, affection and love and that she was being transformed into a spirit fluttering in the sky, radiant with the glow of prophetic inspiration." But disaster strikes; she falls and fractures her shoulder bone. Back home, despite her children's elaborate plans to keep it secret from their father, she confesses to him and begs for forgiveness; her husband, oh so magnanimously, allows her to stay at home until her shoulder heals, and then banishes her! So, even though Mahfouz shows many instances of how confining life in purdah is, in the final analysis he seems to uphold the tradition of masculine control by not voicing or even implying protest. It is like those Hindi movies where the raped woman never gets to marry the right man, however innocent she might be and however chivalrous etcetera he might be in helping her through ordeals. The double jeopardy, double penalty of a masculinist value system *is* often perpetuated unaware.

In contrast to Mahfouz, Rushdie is always aware of how the system subjugates women, and like Ashis Nandy realises that despite this, women are the stronger sex. As he says in an authorial aside in *Shame,* " . . . the women seem to have taken over, they marched in from the peripheries of the story to demand the inclusion of their own tragedies, histories and comedies . . . to see my 'male' plot refracted, so to speak, through the prisms of its reverse and "female' side" (173). Rushdie's women are strong but they are strong despite purdah in the larger sense of the word, despite being systematically and systemically driven to the peripheries.

Each author sets up the central thrust of his/her ideas about purdah in the opening pages of his/her novel.

Rama Mehta's narrative strategies start at the very beginning and work towards the goal that women led an autonomous and complete existence inside the haveli. When her camera pans in, it is directly focused on the women's zenana. If her narrative thrust had been to show the negativity of purdah and "otherness" of women, her camera would have first taken in the men's lavish and modernised quarters before moving onto the women's apartment. Instead, men are the other. "The etiquette established through years permitted only close male relatives to enter the women's apartment. Even so no man entered the courtyard without being properly announced"(4).

Likewise, Attia Hosain's novel begins, "The day my aunt Abida moved from the zenana into the guest-room off the corridor that led to the men's swing of the house . . . " The reference to moving out of the zenana becomes a metaphor. The first pages of both novels also highlight the positive aspects of the system by dwelling on the general security and stability of the zenana and its environs.

Rushdie's *Shame,* too, starts with an impending death that has the same metaphorical associations of change but, unlike the other two novels, the first pages of *Shame* highlight the negative aspects of purdah culture. Unlike Baba Jan and Bhag at Singhji, Old Mr. Shakil is an unrepentant, vile-mouthed reprobate whose three daughters he has "imprisoned in the zenana ring"(13). There are no courtyards with flowers as in *Sunlight* or with colourfully dressed women and canopied altars with chanting priests and festive music as in the *Haveli* (28-29); Nishapur, ironically named after the poetic paradise of another Omar Khayyam, is a fortress more barren than the mountainous landscape around it. Instead of moving out into sunlight as do Laila and Geeta (who, it is implied, will move the entire haveli into the sunlight of education), the Shakil sisters voluntarily barricade themselves by constructing a dumb waiter to cater to all their trade with the outside world, and finally they destroy the entire family. All three novelists make a social statement; Rushdie's statement is that society ought not to condone purdah, not only because it oppresses women but because such oppression unleashes a violence that will destroy all of society. As he says in *Shame,* "Humiliate people for long enough and a wildness bursts out of them" (117).

Rushdie makes only fleeting references to his women characters' costumes. The scene where the women of Q await young Shakil's first public appearance is very visual, and reflexively saw Zeenat, Farida, the washerwomen and other women who had crowded around as being garbed in black or white burqas with the front flap thrown back from their faces. A careful rereading shows that Rushdie himself makes no mention at all of what they are actually wearing. What were Bilquis and Rani and the other women of Bariamma's household wearing? Again, there is no specific evidence for one's reflexive assumption that they wore gararas or salwars or chudidar pyjamas, and that they drew their dupattas over their heads in the presence of men. It is likely that they wore burqas when they went out, given Bariamma's orthodoxy. The dormitory is only Rushdie's characteristic humorous exaggeration for the lack of privacy in a joint family. We know that Bilquis was wearing a costume with a dupatta when her home was burnt to the ground and that her rescuer, Captain Raza, showered her with "blouses, saris, sandals . . . " (66); we know that Pinkie was "in a green sari worn dangerously low upon the hips" (105) and that the socialite women at the parties were definitely not in purdah. But once Raza places his wife under "a kind of unofficial house arrest" (171), "veiling her in walls and shuttered windows" (199), Bilquis does what the Shakil sisters did – she voluntarily goes into purdah, "one morning they all saw Bilquis putting on a black burqa, taking the veil or purdah, even though she was indoors and only family members and servants were present" (208). A little later, we are told that "it [burqa] has never been a difficult garment in that sad house . . . " (219). From these passing references and Maulana Dawood's orthodoxy, we are able to conclude that burqa was a norm in the Hyder household. It is realistic that Raza, Bilquis and Shakil should escape in burqas as their world crumbles around them.

Bilquis's burqas and Rani's shawls are part of Rushdie's arsenal of metaphors. Both sew the burqas and shawls themselves. Whereas Rani's embroidering of Isky's ignominious life-story was intentional, Bilquis's sewing of burqas was intuitive. "I knew I was sewing these for a reason," she says when she brings the burqas so they can escape. Earlier, when Bilquis is questioned about taking the veil, she says, "It was getting too hot, so I wanted to draw the curtains" Step by step Bilquis has been driven into the desert of shame, and she draws the curtains to protect herself from the world. But burqas are always symbols of confinement in *Shame.* The novel is an indictment of the way women have been kept from their place in public and civic life. Unlike the women of the haveli in Mehta's novel and sociological study which narrate the significant role of women in family decisions and through them in political events, the women of Rushdie's *Shame* are denied a central role in both family and public arenas. Bariamma is an exception, but as Mary Daly points out in *Gyn/Ecology* crones are degendered, another kind of erasure of women.

In *Shame,* all the main women, Bilquis, Rani, Shakil Sisters, Arjumand, Pinkie, Naveed, Shahbanou and even Sufiya, are strong but all of them end up scarred and/or misshapen. Denied equal opportunity with men, these women assume Gorgon shapes. Rather than study the scars of private life that might be related to the burqa aspect of purdah, I focus on their isolation, their exclusion from the public sphere.

Bilquis and Rani are prime examples of the injustice and waste wrought by purdah. The first characteristics that teenage Bilquis is given in the novel are that she is a princess and princesses do not serve, and that she is an excellent! actress (5060). Her life turns out otherwise. Her histrionic talents are placed on the back burner not only as possible career but even in private life, and she spends her whole life serving, first Bariamma's household where as the "designated poor thing" she "was given more than her fair share of household duties" (75-76) and then her own household as Raza's wife. Exiled at Q., Bilquis makes a brief foray away from the straight and narrow and is quickly brought to heel when Raza has Sindbad Mengal murdered. True to his reputation as a man "who did not beat his wife" (76), Raza wreaks vengeance only on her lover – and treats Good News Naveed as his own child. But Bilquis's physical isolation at Q. is an externalisation of her separation from Raza's public life. Through the metaphor of clothing Rushdie reiterates his views on history, both Bilquis, and the country's. At Naveed's funeral, Raza Hyder sadly looks at his wife in her black burqa, and thinks, "He saw her history as a slow retreat from that early nudity into the secrecy of the veil" (228). The choice of the word "nudity" rather than "nakedness" is appropriate for the positive and art-centred slant he wishes to give. In the overall context, Bilquis and Naveed are Pakistan, Bilquis its retreat into

Dawoodian conservativism and Naveed its suicidal population explosion.

Rani, whose initial *joie-de-vivre* exceeded Bilquis's, spends most of her life in exile at Mohenjo. She does become a queen, as her name suggests, but her kingdom is far worse than a zenana; it severs her from all public life and any possibility of using her talents and, worse, it does not afford her the security that a zenana gives its residents. Mohenjo is invaded and raped, once by Little Mir and again by Captain Ijjaz and his men. The honourable men of Mehta's haveli are conspicuously absent; indeed the only men on the estate are old and helpless. Iskander visits only rarely; and his visits are just collective orgies. His debauched lifestyle and the new culture of the city comment interestingly enough on the modern transmogrification of the nautch-girl aspect of purdah culture. Whereas in the old system, mistresses usually came from the class of women who were custodians of the arts of entertainment, in the new system, urban society women specialised in the arts of entertainment and became mistresses. Pinkie Aurangzeb and the starlets who visited Q. are examples . . Regrettably, they were worse off than their earlier counterparts in the final count. Pinkie's suicide makes one wonder about Rushdie's feminism. After making a strong positive statement about women who break loose of traditional restraints, Rushdie's decision to have Pinkie commit suicide is problematic, unless it is a historical fact about one of Bhutto's women. On the day of Isky's death, Atiyah Pinkie Aurangazeb hacks out her own heart with a nine-inch knife (106) in a show of loyalty. Rushdie, in his fashion, eulogises the faithfulness of these lovers. Even so, there is little artistic reason for killing off Pinkie in this way, giving her neither the fortresslike power of Rani nor the frightening pathos of Sufiya.

Through expatiating on purdah culture, Rushdie metaphorically inscribes his views about women's isolation in private and public spheres and the consequent loss to society. Sufiya, hidden away from public eye, is an extreme example of the pathos and violence inherent in such isolation; Omar Khayyam's zenana childhood makes him a voyeur while the Shakil Sisters's isolation makes them not only ignorant as children but vindictive crones in their old age. Indeed, not one of the women fulfils her positive potential.

Arjumand Harappa is another prime example of the injustice and waste wrought by purdah. Relegated to her father's shadow because of her gender, she takes on the task of deifying him, "to transmute the preserved fragments of the past into the gold of myth" (181). While the novel successfully develops Rushdie's point about purdah, this is also an example of one of several erroneous judgement-calls that Rushdie has made in his rewriting of history. Whereas for Arjumand "the passage of time eroded her prospects, and at last she ran out of suitors" (182), and her deification of Iskander was personal and without public consequence, Benazir Bhutto's reification of Zulfikar was public and she also went on not only to marry and have children, but to become the prime minister of her country. It is heartening to see real life disproving Rushdie's delineation of women as helplessly imprisoned away from the private and public arenas. That the days of both women-leaders of the sub-continent were numbered and marked by violence, highlights a possibility that feminist and postcolonial radicals might not wish to endorse because it seems so middle-of-the-road, namely, that when discriminatory variables are removed, men and women will not be distinguished by their gender but by their individual propensities for virtues and vices, ambition and contentment, action and passivity oppression and victimisation.

## References

Altetkar, A. S. *The Position of Women in Hindu Civilization.* Motilal Banarsidass, Delhi, 1962.

Gore, M. S. *Urbanization and Family Change,* Bombay: Popular Prakashan 1968.

Hosain, Attia. *Sunlight on a Broken Column.* Delhi: Arnold Heinemann. 1987. First published London: Chatto and Windus.1961.

Kaur, Manmohan. *Role of Women in the Freedom Movement,* Delhi: Sterling Publishers Ltd., 1968.

Lateef, Shahida. *Muslim Women in India.* London: Zed Books. 1990.

Mahfouz, Naguib. *Palace Walk.* New York: Doubleday. 1990.

Mehta, Rama. *Inside the Haveli.* Delhi. Arnold Heinemann, 1977.

– "From Purdah to Modernity" in *Indian Women: From Purdah to Modernity,* ed. B. R. Nanda; see below.

Mujeeb, M. *Islamic Influence of Indian Society.* New Delhi: Meenakshi Prakashan.1972.

Nanda, B. R. ed. *Indian Women: From Purdah to Modernity.* New Delhi: Vikas,1976.

Rushdie, Salman. *Midnight's Children.* London: Pan Books. 1982. First published London: Jonathan Cope, 1981.

– *Shame.* London: Pan Books. 1984. First published London: Jonathan Cape, 1983.

Showalter, Elaine (ed.). *The New Feminist Criticism.* New York: Pantheon. 1985.

Wernher, Hilda. *My Indian Family.* New York: John Day. 1943.

# 13

# The We/They Paradigm in Rushdie's *The Satanic Verses*

Salman Rushdie's *Midnight's Children (1981)* assured him a place as one of the twentieth century's most significant writers in English; the controversy surrounding *The Satanic Verses (1988)* has raised an issue that is crucial, indeed critical, to literary criticism of the New Literatures in English. Literature cannot be divested of its cultural accoutrements, and what we are witnessing is evidence that there are polarities between the Islamic world and the pluralistic world that are equal and opposite. Whereas Rushdie has created a landmark novel out of this tension of opposites, we risk falling into the old trap of comparative value judgements that pit one world-culture against another. Islamic fundamentalism has made the book the centre of a burning controversy, but what has been lost in the explosiveness of terrorist extremism is the fact that the book is

---

This essay was published in US/THEM: *Translation, Transcription and Identity in Post-Colonial Literary Cultures.* Ed: Gordon Collier. Amsterdam: Rodopi. 1992. pp. 189-199. This was originally presented at a conference held in Giessen in 1989 at a time when the Rushdie controversy was still piping hot.

offensive even to moderate Muslims; and, since reverence of the Prophet is a sacred cow in Islam, there is opposition from this world-culture. Further, Islamic governments are non-secular, and make no claim to be otherwise. On the other side, freedom of expression is a sacred cow to our secular world-culture, and we of the democratic world must seek to defend it. However, our problems do not end there, as they would have in the past. In the past, western imperialism had its way, relegating the rest of the world to an inferior status, but today much of the non-Islamic world is avowedly pluralistic, hence must re-examine issues. Pluralism, or multiculturalism as we call it in Canada, is an ideal that is fraught with inbuilt contradictions and controversies because, instead of assuming that there are a number of equal but different cultures, there is an underlying assumption that there is a *majority* culture which allows *minority* cultures to retain their identity. When two sacred cows lock horns, what then? Add to these political opportunism or political expediency, call it what you will, and we get the worldwide conflagration that we have today on this issue.

(I have advisedly used the term "sacred cow" as yet another example of cultural accoutrements in literature. The dictionary defines it as "a belief too sacred to be questioned," and that is the way I use it. The connotative usage of the term, however, tags on denigrating associations of superstition and irrationality, and that is the way some of my colleagues understood it during an oral presentation of this paper, jumping up to say that freedom of expression is not "just a sacred cow." To which my response is: we should use the phrase either denotatively for both concepts-Islamic fundamentalism and democratic ideals of freedom of expression-or connotatively for both; as a Hindu and a New Literatures in English critic, I would advocate that such denigrating connotative usage be thrown out the window altogether.

That is a long parenthetical reference, but one that is essential in the present context of cross-cultural readings of literature.)

This essay is in two parts. In the first part, I have a persona who is an Indian in India responding to the controversy surrounding the banning of *The Satanic Verses* in India. This persona's view is that Rushdie is on the verge of being one-of-them because he seems to have lost touch with political realities in India and with the religion of his fathers. In the second part, I deal with Rushdie's excellent delineation of racism in Britain and how he uses the we-they opposition in developing Saladin Chamcha's evolution into Salahuddin Chamchawala. The second part also responds to the first part's points regarding Rushdie's alienation and excessive use of sexuality.

No, Salman baba, this will not do. Such hopes we had for you, baba, that you will grow onetwothree upupupup but you have let us down, baba, badly let us down. Like Sterne, like Joyce, Garcia Marquez, Borges, we were thinking, and what have you become? a bad copycat of your own worst parts is what. *The Satanic Verses* is bad news, Sal baba, very bad news. Twothree reasons only I will give now though there are many more.

One is: some stories can be written only once, like *Finnegans Wake,* like *Midnight's Children.* Why you didn't learn this from Joyce? *Midnight's C* well done, that's it, khatam. But you, you want to put same old stories in new box, smaller size, bigger price; all stories mixed up, pickled, *GrimusMidnight'sCShame.* Not the cheating I mind, everyone does that, is kaliyuga now. But it is bad taste I can't swallow. Choosing all the worst parts and chutney-mixing everything so the taste is plain awful. Thu, thu, spitting it out is what I did. What anyone can do?

Second thing is not even easy to say, baba. But I must. Because if I don't who will? I have been there all along, baba, read all your stories, even the short one in *The Atlantic Monthly* where you copycatted R.K. Narayan, and I have been praising you sky high, *chand-ka-tukda, chaudhvin-ka-chand-lajawab* etc. etc. So I have to say this now.

This constant fingering of yourself is no good. Three stages in life there be – no pant, half pant and long pant. No pant you do it is okay, Freud and all say theek hai; half pant days you do it, still okay, boys will be boys, chalta hai; but in long pants you do it, no saab, doesn't work. Plain lecher, no soul, no song. Calling on Symbolism, you can try to justify your good self, but writing must hold reader at the literal level first if it is to have any symbolismdimbolism worth. Take this Gibreel-Chamcha hybrid also; is no hybrid at all, no good-evil, no god-shaitan, no

Apollo-Dionysus but only double dose of debauched Dionysus in his cups. What Salahuddin does at end of 547 pages of bildungsroman sweat and anguish? Salah, into bed again, with Zeenat Vakil, and is not only long dead wives can bring libel suits. You can go far and deep, mian, for you have a lot of good things always but I can't understand this obsession with sexual acrobatics (good hakims we have here, janab, if you are having any trouble).

Third point, Salman janab, in *Midnight's C* and *Shame you* were one of us but now I am not so sure. I am hoping you are listening to me with both ears, janab, because I am always being on your side and I don't want to be misunderstood. I was never agreeing with reviewers who said, Who Rushdie thinks he is? what authority he has to write about India and Pakistan sitting khushi-khushi in Vilayat since age 14? I have always been telling, Shut your face, our Salman is one of us, writing from inside because, to sing from his own favourite song, his heart is Hindustanee even if his shoes are Japanee and his clothes Angrezee. But after your *Satanic Verses* what can I do, mian, except hang down my head? I don't say you are one of them, not yet, but you are not here I am saying, you are more there than here, more with them than with us. Everyone knows all human beings are samesame, bhaibhai, but everyone also knows that there's always two sides to a wall with us on one side and them on the other, and that who we and they are depends on who's speaking. Confusion comes when the one who's speaking doesn't know which side he is on. And you, Salman saab, don't know where your good self is standing.

You are confused about what you are meaning to do. One time you tell journalist you are only writing fiction, what the hell only comic fiction; but another time you tell another journalist you are serious, you spend five years studying Islam, you have never been more serious you are saying. You are confused about who you want to be. You want to be angrez when in India looking down your nose at students for buying pirated copy and talking down at them, but you want to be desi in your fiction taking up and all for your countrymen. Like poor Chamcha you are being, good and proper angrez but you can't break free of us.

You are confused about whom you are writing for. After *Shame* you said you were khatam-finished with India Pakistan as setting but what happened? You are still writing about India-in-India, India-in-England, Indians-in-India, Indians-in-England. You can't write about anything else, mian, we are your bread and butter, and you with your angrez-trained mind know which side your bread is buttered. But learn from your own Gibreel that only we will stand by you. The angrez now join you in your loudloud badnattli-abuse of book banning but we only are your best readers and call you chand-ka-tukda, farishta mian. That is why I am being so sad, Salman, why you didn't see what was coming? That is why I am afraid you are not quite one of us. How else to explain your misjudgement, mian? It breaks my heart to see you hidinghiding and all this blood and fire; but the moment you told Rajivbhai that banning book was like putting victim in prison instead of educating attacker, I said, Hai Ram, our Salman has lost touch with his native land and with the religion of his fathers. And now look at you, mian, your book is free but you are in worse than prison and a price upon your head.

I was no great admirer of Rajivbhai, Salman mian, and I am no believer in your Prophet, but I am clearly understanding why the book was being banned. Two reasons I am giving. One, politicians are always using the religion to divide and rule, divide and rule, and if they can't rule, be dog in manger and divide anyway. In Angrezi Raj it was Hindus set up against Muslims; in Partition time it was Sikhs versus Muslims; Muslims versus non-Muslims; in Bangladesh it was Bengali Muslims against Punjabi Muslims; more recently it is being like forest fire, mian: Hindus vs Sikhs, Hindus vs Muslims, one Hindu caste vs other Hindu caste. Salman mian, why you don't know that the communalism kills more people in India than oldage plus cars plus drugs in Amreeka? Is easy for you to tell Rajivbhai to educate people instead of banning book bit janab, pocket your ego and be practical. Is not for nothing Marx said religion is opium of people except that he got drug wrong is not opium but LSD/heroin, hard stuff that puts scorpions in brain. If fanatic fathers like Shahabuddin give imported matches to children, tell me which is better way to prevent the fires? to confiscate matches or let the Rome burn while you are educating such fathers and children?

Second reason why book is banned, Salman mian don't get angry, if friends like me can't say who can? is because you are being pigheaded. Anyone can see your Mahound story is in bad taste, much worse even than your pigheaded reference to Indiraji by name in *Midnight's C.* You pulled off the serious-comic coupling in earlier books but are falling flat on your face in *The Satanic Verses.* As simple as that. Not your day. Got up on wrong side of bed. Not up to par. Probably because you really truly want to make a serious statement on Islam in a serious way but you can't get away from your juvenile infatuation with erotica. I can't understand your misjudgement, baba, I have tried and tried but all I can come up with is that you have lost touch with your native land and with the religion of your fathers. Your native land will forgive and remember you as a favourite son, baba, but the religion of your fathers? Salman baba, what can I say? I know my history. I know about all the Muhammads who came to our land, Ghazni and Ghori and bin Tughlak to name only the bestknown, and I know what drove them and how they drove others. Mad, madder, maddest every one of them spreading the creed at sword point. Only a handful among a billion moderates yes, but I know our history, baba, how could you forget it? Just as Salahuddin made up with his father, will you ever be able to make up? I don't think so, baba, this father is not like Chamchawala and also there are too many fathers just like your Omar Shakil had too many mothers. My heart goes tharrap tharrap for your safety, baba, and is not good news that your new countrymen know they are paying a thousand pounds a day on your security. You think maybe new face would be helping? plastic surgery and new passport and some hair on your head? Baba, baba, maybe Mary Pereira could switch you like she did Saleem? maybe Reverend Mother could swaddle you in perforated sheet? maybe Bariamma could hide you in her impregnable dormitory and you surely would like that if you were like your creations. Maybe Flapping Eagle could show you hole in Mediterranean to go to another Dimension? Salman baba, my heart it is going tharrap tharrap.

* * * * * *

To turn from Indian English to a drier dialect, there are, as I said, two parts to this essay. One is that Rushdie's error of judgement makes one tend to the view that he is not-one-of-us-Indians but one of them "emig-runts," as Haji Sufyan says; the second is that Rushdie's delineation of the status and ethos of Indians-in-Britain and of British racism is so insightful, so excellent that one tends to think that he is certainly one-of-us-Indians as different from one-of-them-Angrez.

To the first part, I would like to add two brief points. *The Satanic Verses* contains passages which clearly indicate that Rushdie knew the subject matter of his novel is volatile; Rushdie did not err in kind but erred in his assessment of the degree of volatility and the degree of reactionary violence.

There are numerous examples to show that Rushdie knew he would rouse the ire of a large number of people. Salman the Persian and Baal the Poet are two of his spokesmen. So that his own name could play a part in the aspersions implied in the Prophet's failure to recognize that his words had been changed, Rushdie combines the identity of two historical figures-Salman the Persian and Abdullah ibn abi Sarh, who was one of Prophet Muhammad's amanuenses and is said to have falsified records. Rushdie also uses historically recorded incidents of how Abu Sufyan (named Àbu Simbel in the novel) and Hind enlisted writers to lampoon the Prophet. Towards the end, Baal makes fun of Mahound by declaiming about his own marriage to the twelve replica-wives of the Prophet in The Curtain, and Baal is beheaded. Baal's betrayer is, curiously enough, Salman, whom Khalid would dearly have loved to behead. But Salman blubbers and whimpers and pleads, "swears renewed loyalty," and then betrays Baal in exchange for his own life.

There is an ironic dimension to the number of instances where Rushdie has partially prophesied his own future. When Farishta starts production on his satanic version of the Ramayana with Ravana the demon-king portrayed as the good force and Rama the god-king as the evil force, George says: "looks like he's trying deliberately to set up a final confrontation with religious sectarians, knowing he can't win, that he'll be broken into bits"

(*Satanic Verses* 539). Rushdie, in his usual flamboyant manner, pokes fun at communal hysteria generated by religious bigots. Unfortunately, he has chosen the wrong religion unlike Farishta, who chose Hinduism as the medium for his message about public outcry. Slandering India's majority religion would have been a silent flop, ignored and soon forgotten as was Farishta's production; the acceptance of the many misrepresentations that occur in the current television series on the epics (which series probably prompted Rushdie's reference) is a living example of how India's majority religion can be maligned and misrepresented with impunity. But the slandering of Islam is another matter altogether; and however ingenious Rushdie's conception of moulding the Mahound segment into a movie production, given the various combinations of fundamentalists, opportunists and terrorists in the political context, and given the global strength of Islam, the violence of reaction is predictable.

To go on to the second part, there are several pairs of we-they pairings in *The Satanic Verses;* and, through the technique of montage, Rushdie manages to cover a wide range of groups and types. However, most of the pairs may be categorized under two major headings: the we-they interaction within the emigration-immigration paradigm, and the insider-outsider perspectives within the framework of religious beliefs. These two are parallel developments and, though the latter has been highlighted in the controversy surrounding the book, the former is more hard-hitting, realistic and offensive; and it is the emigration immigration paradigm that I shall consider here.

There are three sets of we-they pairings involving those who move from one country to another: Indian emigrants are seen as "they" by Indians who do not emigrate but live in India; native-born white Britons see immigrants, especially from Asia, as "they"; Asian immigrants in Britain form their own sense of ethos, and consider others in Britain as "they." Saladin Chamcha is in each of the three categories at different times in the novel.

Through the Zeenat-Saladin relationship, Rushdie delineates how each side views the other in India. At the beginning of the novel, Saladin consciously distances himself from Indians in India; Zeenat Vakil teases him about his desire to disown India and his unconscious bonding, which draws him to his roots. She feels his salvation lies in his recognition and acceptance of this bonding. The novel ends with Saladin taking this step towards wholeness, when he goes with Zeenat, who has clearly become a symbol of this deep core of identity.

In Britain, Saladin aligns himself with white native-born Englishmen; he is chagrined and mortified when immigration officers treat him as an alien; he goes through a learning process, slowly re-aligning himself with Indians in Britain and, still later, with Indians-in-India. Through and behind all this is Salman Rushdie, whose heart is Hindustanee and who therefore can portray the world of Shaandaar Cafe and of Chamchawala Sr. with uncensored accuracy without losing his readers' sympathy for that world. One has only to compare V.S. Naipaul's *An Area of Darkness* with Rushdie's portrayal of Brickhall and Bombay to see how two authors can deal with the same scene and yet convey two entirely different experiences. The easiest way to explain this difference in writer-response is to say that Naipaul hates, or finds repugnant, what he shows and sees, whereas Rushdie has affection for what he sees and shows. One discerns the same difference between Ruth Prawer Jhabvala's fiction and Arun Joshi's or Manohar Malgonkar's; between the many movies that unduly romanticize or denigrate Indian life, and Mira Nair's *Salaam Bombay!*

Rushdie says many relevant and insightful things about the immigrant ethos. About the baggage that the immigrant brings with him, which weighs him down; about prejudice within the British immigration department, which abuses and abases non-white residents; about the riots in Brixton (which he calls Brickhall); about police brutality, such as has been happening in Canada as well. The main narrative techniques to note are: that Rushdie's omissions are as important as what he includes; that he deals directly with issues through authorial commentary; and that he shows the nuances of these issues more indirectly and more powerfully through Saladin Chamcha's journey of self-discovery. One could say with Angel Gibreel that Saladin and Salman Rushdie are one and the same: "It was me both times, baba, me first and second also me" (123); but there is a distinction.

The omniscient narrator is forthright in his condemnation of racist immigration policies in Britain. Very early in the novel, he describes some familiar ways in which immigration officers harass incoming and returning immigrants. In order to verify that immigrants were not being smuggled in through unconsummated marriages of convenience, where phony spouses get sponsored into the country and then go their separate ways, officers grill them with personal questions. Rushdie succinctly refers to this practice when he describes the passengers on the jumbo jet *Bostan:*

> there had been more than a few migrants aboard, yes, quite a quantity of wives who had been grilled by reasonable, doing-their-job officials about the length of and distinguishing moles upon their husband's genitalia, a sufficiency of children upon whose legitimacy the British government had cast its ever-reasonable doubts. [4]

The sarcasm of repeating the word "reasonable" is unmistakable. A few lines later, he once again shows the we-English point of view about they-the immigrants:

> Just two brown men, falling hard, nothing so new about that you may think; climbed too high, got above themselves, flew too close to the sun, is that it? [5]

The Icarus allusion is slanted by his syntax, with the phrase "got above themselves" referring back to the brownness of the men and so reducing the grave mythic associations of the Icarus story.

For Saladin, Icarus is a very appropriate allusion; at the beginning of the novel he has aspired to fly close to the English sun. He has striven hard

> to become the thing his father was-not-could-never-be, that is, a goodandproper Englishman . . . even if his classmates giggled at his voice and excluded him from their secrets, because these exclusions only increased his determination, and that was when he began to act, to find masks that these fellows would recognize, paleface masks, clown masks, until he fooled them into thinking he was okay, he was *people-like-us.* He fooled them the way a sensitive human

> being can persuade gorillas to accept him into their family, to fondle and caress and stuff bananas in his mouth. [43]

Note Rushdie's "inversion" of equating the whites with gorillas and brown Saladin with humans. Chamcha has been a victim of racism since his early days in England, but has combatted it on the Englishmen's terms, suppressing and disguising his differentness. Rushdie calls this a learning process:

> most migrants learn, and can become disguises. Our own false descriptions to counter the falsehoods invented about us, concealing for reasons of security our secret selves. [49]

To the Icarus allusion is added another series of allusions, which forms a refrain as the novel progresses and connects Chamcha to Farishta:

> To be born again, first *you* have to die . . . Phoenix-from-ashes, the resurrection of Christ, the transmigration at the instant of death, of the *soul* of the Dalai Lama into the body of a newborn child. *[84]*

Saladin dies several times and rises renewed. His first death was in an early incident which Rushdie singled out in one of his television interviews. On his first day at breakfast at the English public school, he sees a kipper on his plate and, in his ignorance, eats a mouthful of bones. Not one of his fellow-students helps him out.

> Then the thought occurred to him that he had been taught an important lesson. England was a peculiar-tasting smoked fish full of spikes and bones, and nobody would ever tell him how to eat it. [44]

He vows that he will "show them." Chamcha shows them by becoming one of them. But Rushdie, looking over Chamcha's shoulder when Chamcha is still one of them, shows how British racism works. When describing the hunt for illegal aliens on the beach, he couples the cops and dogs in an image that animalizes the humans: "Fifty-seven beachcombers were accompanied by thirteen dogs, all sniffing the sea air and lifting excited legs"

(139). Note that the cops, too, are lifting their legs, not just the dogs.

Later, while Chamcha metamorphoses into a goat, the police and immigration officers are shown to be more brutish than he. He is still naive:

> "This isn't England," he thought, not for the first or last time. How could it be, after all; where in all that moderate and common-sensical land was there room for such a police van in whose interior such events as these might plausibly transpire? [158]

He is treated like an animal. "'You're all the same," says one of the policemen as he beats him up. "Can't expect animals to observe civilized standards" (159). His computerized credentials are cast in doubt: "Who're you trying to kid? . . . Look at yourself. You're a fucking Packy billy" (163). But Rushdie, looking over Saladin's shoulder, consistently develops the connection between animals and human beings as one in which the animals are superior. The choice of a caprine incarnation for the "demi-goat" Saladin is related to William Blake's proverb of hell: the lust of the goat is the bounty of God.

Blake's proverb can explain Rushdie's excessive use of sexuality. Rushdie admires Blake, and part of his inspiration reflects Blake's. Indeed, one feels that Rushdie's litany of England's evils comes from the same source as Blake's "London" – a genuine and deep-seated love for the country and genuine pain at its corruption. This authenticity of emotion is what makes Saladin's journey of self-discovery so anguishing for himself and for us.

Like Blake's Albion, England is fallen, and Rushdie exploits the same sexual relationships as poets and seers have used for centuries. Saladin, incarcerated in a hospital,

> found himself dreaming of the Queen of making tender love to the Monarch. She was the body of Britain, the avatar of the State, and he had chosen her, joined with her; she was his Beloved, the moon of his delight. [169]

Like many of those allusions of Rushdie's that have their source in the current news media, this one probably derives from the incident a few years ago when a man sneaked into the Queen's bedroom; but Rushdie always enriches his sources, combining here the two metaphoric traditions of the body politic and of Eastern love poetry.

Elsewhere, in a long interior monologue, Saladin reflects on his feelings for England (397-405), employing the same images of merger through union: he had given his love to this city, London ... had been creeping up on it, stealthily, with mounting excitement . . . dreaming of being the one to possess it and so . . . *become* it. [398]

It is significant that Rushdie uses a childhood game here and elsewhere; that factor, too, might explain the juvenile quality of much of his erotica.

Rushdie develops the story of Saladin's arrest to give specific examples of police brutality. The authorities conspire to falsify evidence:

> "Seems you were that sick, you did pass out on us after all. Nine of us remember *it* well. I suggest, Mr. Citizen Saladin, that *you* dinna trouble with a complaint." [167]

The omniscient narrator – unlike Saladin's consciousness, which sometimes registers but at other times forgets the injustices – is direct in his recording of racist incidents. Rushdie uses the technique of amassing a load of information, packing the paragraph with details that cumulatively build up a barrage of irrefutable evidence of racism. What he omits is (I repeat) as important as what he includes. For example, he excludes all reference to white victims, so that the effect is not one of indiscriminate or universal brutality but of police brutality against non-whites. The two messages, of brutality per se and of racism, are very different; and Rushdie's selectivity here is significant.

Saladin, like many Indian immigrants, has dissociated himself from his origins. Hal Valance's obnoxious declamation and Saladin's response to him are sickening but realistic. Valance says there is racism in society, and he will go along with it because he is a salesman and the customer is always right. He says how he has reshaped his advertising expertise in the light of racism; he excludes Blacks from his commercials, re-records a jingle because the company chairman "'thought the singer sounded, black," and acquiesces to an airline company that has stated categorically that they do not want Blacks in their ads. Saladin's response is: "I've never felt I belonged to a race"; and he gets the job. While it may be true that this rootlessness is both a boon and a bane to immigrants, to say so at this juncture is opportunistic treachery.

Saladin has never aligned himself with Indians; but being forced to do so is a step forward in self-discovery. When Jumpy Joshi brings him to Haji Sufyan's *Bed and Breakfast Shaandaar Cafe,* gentle Sufyan welcomes him, saying: "Where else would you go to heal your disfigurements and recover your normal health? Where else but here, with us, among your own people, your own kind?" (253). That again is a realistic touch, depicting how Indian immigrants form their own sense of community, their own ethos Rushdie enumerates several racist incidents through the reports of such characters as Pamela Chamcha, who is a deputy community-relations officer:

Last week a respected Asian street trader . . . was deported after eighteen years in Britain because, fifteen years ago, he posted a certain form forty eight hours late. Next week . . . the police will be trying to fit up a fifty-year-old Nigerian woman, accusing her of assault, having previously beaten her senseless. [183]

The chapter "Angel Azraeel" is packed with similar passages. For example:

> Stories of police brutality, of black youths hauled swiftly into unmarked cars and vans . . . and flung out, equally discreetly, covered in cuts and bruises, spread throughout the communities. [451]

Through Saladin and his authorial commentary, Rushdie draws two interconnected circles. One is that Saladin's final rebirth takes him back to India. Reconciled with his dying father, made immensely rich by his inheritance (his walnut tree and material possessions are both symbolic of sense, and of his place of belonging), and drawn by love towards Zeenat Vakil, Salahuddin Chamchawala comes full circle, back to his native land. It is implied that the core of Indianness in him which Zeeny sought to save will probably be redeemed and nurtured after all. Saladin reverts from emigrant to exile to repatriate. Exile, Rushdie expounds, is very different from immigration. "Exile is a dream of glorious return," Rushdie has the Imam muse (205). Saladin does not stay too long in a state of exile. It may even be said that he recognizes only after his repatriation that he has been an exile nourishing a dream of glorious return.

The other circle relates to England. Saladin returns to India, but a host of Indian immigrants are in Britain and other western countries to stay; the we-they conflict will go on for a long time; however, I read yet another prophecy in Rushdie's novel. He sees non-white immigrants coming into their own, and I see them going further-I see them taking over these countries.

In *Shame,* Rushdie says that there comes a point in the building-up of inner shame when violence takes over and changes things in its own way. In *The Satanic Verses,* the manticore in the hospital says likewise: "'some of us aren't going to stand for it. We're going to bust out of here before they turn us into anything worse." The manticore realizes that he has been victimized and moulded: "They describe us . . . . That's all. They have the power of description, and we succumb to the pictures they construct" (168).

I see a fantasy follow-up sequence that Rushdie has not developed. There is an echo from *Shame* in *The Satanic Verses.* At the hospital where Saladin is detained, he hears a woman in labour:

> and at intervals ranging from fifteen to thirty minutes for what seemed like an endless time she continued to add new babies to the already improbable numbers marching, like conquering armies, from her womb. [166]

Saladin also gets ... "a rich aroma similar to that of exotic spices sizzling in clarified butter-coriander, turmeric, cinnamon, cardamom, cloves." Rushdie is using these images of endless procreation and aromas for the same effect as in *Shame* and *Midnight's Children* respectively. Good News's fertility and Shiva's potency are symptomatic of population-boom. Outside Asia, the South Asian population is growing much faster than the white population. The masalas of India have found their way to all corners of the globe. This surely is. a prophecy based on sound statistical projection. *Time* and *Newsweek* have had cover stories on the superior achievement-levels of Asian students in the United States and on the growing illiteracy of students in general; I will not draw any conclusions on *IQs per se;* but history shows that the phenomena of political and cultural domination move in waves. In my fantasy, the conquering armies marching from immigrant and Asian wombs will out-number, out-think and outshine the others and take over. Not an unfit retribution for the races that have annihilated aboriginal cultures and peoples in five continents over the past five hundred years.

## Works Cited

Rushdie, Salman. *1988. The Satanic Verses.* London and New York: Viking.

# 14

# A Review of a Text

Memuna. *The Deaths of Sullyman Rush-to-Die*. Toronto: Celestial Publishing. 1991. 178pp

Salman Rushdie opened the floodgates of inspiration for a whole generation of writers with his *Midnight's Children*. His free-flowing, colloquial prose-style and his combination of irreverent abandon with high seriousness of tone are echoed in various recent South Asian Canadian fiction. It started with M.G. Vasanji's *The Gunny Sack* (1989). Now we have two other volumes, one rather too close for comfort to Rushdie! Some of the episodes in the life/lives of Memuna's Sullyman resemble Salman's, but of course this is a work of fiction and we find the usual disclaimer, "any reference to persons dead or alive is unintentional." So the parallels I draw are mine, not the author's.

---

Author's Note: I include my review of Memuna's book because I find it an interesting spin-off of the Rushdie Affair. I tried to find out more about the author, but all I could discover at the time was that she was a woman in her fifties who lives in Canada. It seems as though the author has got an insight into what makes Rushdie tick, and there are serendipitous prophecies where Sullyman finds solace in Maya's jet black hair. This was a review of two books, the other being Yasmin Ladha's *Lion's Granddaughter and Other Stories*. The review appeared in *Toronto South Asian Review*.)

Each of the twenty-five chapters is a story, an episode that is not connected to the preceding or following one. However, the key characters recur often enough to give a backbone of continuity. Sullyman, an Indian Muslim is married to Janice, a white woman who tries to comfort and shield him from the predators outside their home and from himself; but she cannot stop him having his nightmares. As he rinses his mouth, a tooth falls off, and then another and another, and then his hair, ear, nose, eyeballs. Do you hear echoes of Saleem's voice and words? I do, but that is only because I am an obsessive critic of Salman R. More seriously, my criterion of a "good read" is that it makes the reviewer imitate the author's style; the last time it happened was quite a while ago – when I reviewed Kamala Markandaya's *The Pleasure City*.

Sullyman's wife is Janice, white and well-bred. And then there is Priya, not free-mouthed like Zeenat Vakil, but as magnetic and intelligent. She discusses hybridity, incipient racism in Canada and the U.S., and the many problems of the matrimonial state. "But it was Maya he wanted and needed." Maya of black hair and black eyes. Maya is just that, an illusion, elusive but always there for him, a spirit perhaps of India? in whose sea of jet black hair he can lose himself and forget that he is a marked man who has to die. Sullyman dies repeatedly in the volume, once shot by Priya, once in Tianenmen Square, once as he watches his grandmother's death, once buried alive by those who had never read his book but are convinced it is a Christian plot to undermine Islam. Of all the numerous characters, Talib is the most significant. Sullyman and Talib discuss religion, his predicaments, his options; they analyze Islam from various angles. But at one point, even Talib turns against him, "Why, you bag of dirt! You had me fooled. So you did it for money after all. Who paid you? Who's in it this time, the Americans, the Europeans or the Russians?"

The narrative holds one's attention, even though Uska Dada's stories do not always make connections with the rest. However, it is most unfortunate that the typescript seems not to have had the benefit of an editor to clean up such errors as "her's" for "hers" and "it's" for "its."

Also, I feel some regret that it was not picked up by a better-known publisher.

# 15

# Dancing Through the Minefield Called Salman Rushdie

It is a pleasure and honour to be here.

I have chosen to speak informally on a general topic rather than formally on a specific topic. The reason is simple: the work on Rushdie is so prolific, and increasing so rapidly, that only a doctoral candidate is likely to have the latest developments on his fingertips, and only other doctoral candidates are likely to be interested in deep and detailed analyses. However, all of us are familiar with Salman Rushdie's work and interested in it, and therefore I decided on focusing my talk around the potentials and pitfalls of Rushdie studies, and on some ideas on topics and approaches to teaching and criticism that wait to be explored.

I started my research career studying Indo-English literature; then I went on to spend several years on other postcolonial literatures; then I was immersed in Rushdie for about a decade,

---

I was external examiner for Joel Kuorrti's Ph.D. dissertation on Salman Rushdie's fiction. It was a formal and public event, with students, thesis supervisor and Opponent, as my position was called, in academic robes. Later, I had to give a talk, and I prepared this for that occasion. As an interesting trivia, the department had asked the police and university security to be on alert, in case the topic of the dissertation roused any disturbance among students or townspeople. The talk was given on Thursday, October 8, 1998.

starting in 1981; more recently, I have gone on to other things, spending about five years on women's literature, and now I am engaged in the literature of the Indian diaspora, having come full circle back to my Indian origins and everyday Diaspora realities. During my Rushdie phase, I had charted a great many avenues of exploration; in the course of this talk, I thought I would pass on a few of the research ideas that I did not develop to any publishable depth, and to talk about my teaching experiences in this area.

There are several points I wish to make about the impact of Rushdie's writing.

**One**

Rushdie opened up the English language, and sent it soaring. To give just one aspect of this, earlier writers from the Asian and African wings of the empire used to include glossaries to explicate vernacular words and idioms; Rushdie's immediate predecessors, such as Chinua Achebe, for example, explained their vernacular terms within the body of the text. Rushdie, on the other hand, has used Indian and Indianised terminology without explication and thus has expanded the frontiers of the English language. Through this he has reiterated that the English language must and can reflect linguistic and cultural diversity, and English I think has always been amenable to such expansion. If so many writers of the Indian diaspora have gained recognition in recent times, it is thanks to Rushdie who taught the west how to read both the metaphorical language and the linguistic acrobatics of improvisation of the Diaspora writer.

There is another side to every coin. There is, I believe, a price that these writers have paid for their expertise; I do not say the price was not worth paying, but only that we have to be aware that every coin has two sides. I mentioned that I am now studying Diaspora writers. One of my ongoing research topics is that some of the more successful writers have enough power over language dexterously to suggest the range and depth of cultural idiosyncrasies but they can go so far and no further, and that there is in an inevitable disjunction of what I call sensibility or ethos. I usually cite Bharati Mukherjee as a prime example of this mastery over language on one hand and a serious flaw of sensibility on the other. From the publication of *Jasmine* in 1991, through *The Middleman and Other Stories* in 1992, The *Holder of the World* in 1994, and *Leave it to Me* in 1997, her sensibility has progressively deteriorated though her control over language is as strong as ever. Her works are enthusiastically praised outside India, as evinced by the number of awards and recognition she has received, and as forcefully denigrated in India and among the Diaspora. The disparity of response is one of my present areas of study. I am now inclined to think that Rushdie too falls under the same category of superb language manipulation and rather questionable sensibility. I hope he will come through this. More of this aspect of Rushdie later.

**Two**

Just as Rushdie opened up the linguistic arena to Diaspora writers, he opened up the critical arena to Diaspora critics. What started off as a "counterpoint" or counter voice within the imperial discourse soon became a full-fledged counter-discourse. Within five years of *The Satanic Verses,* we had major break-throughs in literary theory made by post-colonial critics, many of whom are of the Diaspora. To name just a few of the critical volumes that have become an indispensable part of any post-colonial critical collection, we have Gauri Viswanathan's *Masks of Conquests (1989),* Aijaz Ahmad's *In Theory,* Javed Majeed's *Ungoverned Imaginings,* Partha Chatterji's *The Nation and Its Fragments,* all in *1992,* Homi Bhabha's *Location of Culture* in 1994.

These critics have changed the course of criticism, questioning Edward Said, (indeed Aijaz Ahmad all but overthrows Said,) and freeing theory from its imperialistic anchor to give it its own moorings. By that I mean that whereas colonial expansion, order, oppressions, were the reference points earlier, now these referents are giving way to more current political realities and it is time to stop flogging the dead horse of imperialism. The new critics are critical of the pioneers, including of Gayatri Spivak and the subaltern group, for example.

Years ago, I thought of the distinction between the words "half-breed" and "cross-breed," as an addition to my lexicon. Whereas "half-breed" has strong negative connotations of inferiority the word "cross-breed," because of its associations with botanical and genetic breeding contexts, has a strong positive connotation, as a process by which a species takes on the best of two different genetic strains to form a tougher, more resistant and resilient strain. In the title poem of my first collection, written in the early seventies, I have the lines, "who frowned on cross-breeding black and white/But not the miscegenation of cultures/White and brown."

The present term for this concept of mine is the term "hybridity," and critics such as Homi Bhabha in *The Location of Culture* (1994) have formulated their critical theory around the concept. Just as Edward Said started a movement that has gone far beyond the parameters of his own theory, Rushdie's novels and essays gave impetus to an efflorescence that goes far beyond what he ever espoused or would endorse.

Three, in feminist discourse we often quote Adrienne Rich's words, "The personal is political." The reception of Rushdie's *The Satanic Verses* has shown that one could well say "the religious is political;" religion and politics intersect at a personal and inescapable level in the Indian sub-continent and this is something that the west generally responds to in a rather Orientalist manner; there is a deep divide between the western and non-western political milieu, the import of which the western nations have not quite comprehended. (Mr. Kuorrti's earlier book on *The Satanic Verses,* which he has aptly titled *The Place of the Sacred,* shows that Mr. Kuorrti is far more sensitive to this issue than most other western critics.)

The controversy over *The Satanic Verses* has shown the strength of the pan-Islamic movement in today's world. I repeat, the western nations have not quite grasped the import of the spread of this pan-Islamic movement and they had better do so if they have to function effectively in the political arena. Just as the missionary zeal of Christianity, aided by colonial guns, spread its imperial wings over the world and transformed world culture, the contemporary thrust of Islam, aided by the economic wealth of oil, is expanding by leaps and bounds, and is poised to change the world in as spectacular and unequivocal a manner as Christianity and colonialism did. The official fatwah on Rushdie has recently been withdrawn, as we know, but dissidents will always be in danger in the new world order that this movement envisages.

My fourth point is something that I have been mulling over ever since I worked on the paper that I presented at Giessen in 1989 titled, "The We-They Paradigm in Rushdie's *The Satanic Verses.*" In that paper, I argue that Rushdie is one of "us," a spokesperson for the colonized and the immigrant, as against one of "them," the Eurocentric imperialists. However, now I am leaning towards a contrapuntal viewpoint which I presented through an Indian voice in the introduction to that paper. This persona is an Indian in India responding in Indian-English to the controversy surrounding the banning of *The Satanic Verses,* and this persona's view is that Rushdie has lost touch with political realities in India and with the religion of his fathers.

Let me read the relevant paragraphs from that paper. *(see previous essay)*

Annette Kolodny has an interesting essay on the theory, practice and politics of feminist literary criticism; she titles it, "Dancing through the Minefield." This would be an appropriate title for Rushdie studies as well.

My book, *The Perforated Sheet: Essays on Salman Rushdie's Art,* was published in India in 1988, and of course did not include *The Satanic Verses,* which had been released in September, just before or just after, my book had rolled off the press. My publisher did not do much promotional work for my book, as you may well imagine. He decided that dancing through the minefield was beyond his line of duty.

A classroom experience at the time was another dance. In the early nineties, we had a group of students from Malaysia on a special programme, and Commonwealth Literature was one of the courses in their requirement. I had Rushdie's *Shame* on the textbook list. One day, a student told me she would not buy or read the book. I respected her for standing up for her beliefs. I said I could see her reservations, and I opened up the topic for discussion so that we could decide democratically. Very few spoke up, and for me it was an interesting experience in cross-cultural communication.

A few days ago, I found that one does not have to go too far to find that Rushdie is considered a minefield to be avoided. A young man I had never seen before came into my office just three weeks ago, and talked about his interests in the literature of the Diaspora; he spoke enthusiastically about a Bangladeshi writer in Australia, and of some of the activist writers in Canada. He said he is a Muslim, born in Canada of Pakistani parents, and that he is an honours student in our department; as we discussed, I was impressed by his reading repertoire. But when I asked about his ideas on Rushdie, he said flat out that he had not and is not likely to read Rushdie, since he is a practising Muslim. I was not surprised at the views of a visiting student from Malaysia who was soon returning to her country, but I was quite surprised that a Canadian-born young man should hold the same view, which is really a pity because it seems like those who can understand the nuances refuse to read him and those who don't have the cultural background to read between the lines are the ones taking on the task of studying him in classrooms.

The experience of presenting that paper at Giessen was quite memorable for me because, you will recall, summer 1989 was the time when the controversy was erupting internationally following the *fatwah.* I won't go into why the conference was memorable, since it has no place in the present context, but let me give you an example of how one can get paranoid in such a situation. In the summer of 1991, I got a phone call from a female voice that said she had read all of my works on Rushdie, and would like to meet with me. I reacted with some hesitation, as you may well imagine. Rushdie's Italian translator had recently been attacked, and his Japanese translator had been killed.

However, I decided that since I was already dancing through the minefield, I might as well meet this caller, and that is how I met Linda, who soon became my research assistant.

We wanted to study how Robyn Davidson and Salman Rushdie, Marianne Wiggins and Salman Rushdie, who were lovers in real life, appeared in each other's writing. As a preamble to the study, we started looking at other literary pairs, such as Elizabeth Barrett and Robert Browning, Simone de Beauvoir and Jean Paul Sartre. One pair led to another and we found ourselves swarmed by a Pandora's box of lovers and ex-lovers sufficient to keep us in the pool for several years. At that time, I was chairing a project on women-focused research; and I got side-tracked from Rushdie/Davidson into studying

Canadian writer Elizabeth Smart, who had a long-standing liaison with British novelist George Barker. The paper that came of it was "Real Life Lovers in Each Other's Fiction" in which we substantiated our thesis that whereas women writers are generous in their memories of their ex-lovers, and celebrate the positives, men, if at all they write about their own liaisons, tend towards self justification and self-exoneration which sometimes stretches to negate or disown their shared passions.

I don't think I shall ever return to the topic of Davidson and Rushdie or Wiggins and Rushdie, but I hope someone else will.

During the course of my conversations with my Linda, I realized that she and I came to Rushdie from entirely different positions. Trying to figure out why, I first linked it to sheer individual differences in reading preferences. Then I thought it could be a cross-cultural phenomenon.

Some years ago, at The Writers' Union of Canada, we had a rather heated year of discussion on Voice Appropriation and what needed to be done to give fair space to First Nations and minority groups in the literary world. The burning issue was "Who can write for or about Whom?" In deference to the Renaissance of the First Nations that we were and are experiencing in Canada, I agreed with the Racial Minority members position that all non-Natives should keep their literary hands off Native cultural property, though for all others, I thought an author should be judged by how well the material was handled rather than by the author's blood lineage.

Applied to Rushdie, the point has been made by several Muslim critics that Muslims are the best judges of Rushdie's *The Satanic Verses.* I don't agree, given my stated position. However, during my conversations with Linda, I did wonder as to who the Insider is? Re: the point that Muslims are the best judges of Rushdie's *The Satanic Verses,* that only insiders can truly comprehend the import of his handling of the sacred texts, So who is an Insider? Someone who knows the Indian sub-continent and Islam even if they don't have the literary expertise to get the resonances of Rushdie's intertextuality, or someone who knows how to read literature though they do not have any experience of the sub-continent and culture? This, if you think on it, is one of the main bones of contention in the controversy over *The Satanic Verses.*

I think those who have lived in the subcontinent can enjoy the humour and satire better than those who have never lived there. As Sean O'Faolain says, it is the pleasure of recognition that makes the text come alive. Of course I am very partisan in that I have personally lived the years of *Midnight's Children.* For me, Rushdie first and foremost means the marvellous joys of reading, the sheer hilarity of the narrative and style; for example, what better way to treat sexuality than to exaggerate and laugh at it? But Linda read Rushdie very differently. While she went on methodically to document autobiographical elements and magic realism and psychoanalytic readings of Rushdie's dysfunctional families and magicians' ghettoes and obsession about houses and parents, I sat shaking my head in despair. Joint families under patriarchs and matriarchs can get insanely chaotic, but to call them dysfunctional? Those rambling houses that Rushdie has in every novel could be seen as horror chambers of Rushdie's neuroses in a psychoanalytic reading, but I have lived in them, and all that Rushdie does is exaggerate it, seeing with a slight angle to reality, as he says. As a child, I lived with my parents, five siblings, a houseful of servants, and a cousin or guest at any given time, in a house that I remembered as huge. In the summers, we used to sleep on cots on the front lawn, under the stars and clouds, and it was of course spooky if one read as I did, murder mysteries, Gothic and vampire fantasies. The week I was reading *Dracula,* I remember insisting on having a mosquito curtain around my bed as we slept under the sky, because I wanted that net of security between me and the vampire !!! When my daughter was twelve, the age I had been when I read *Dracula,* I took her to India and visited my old home town, and of course the house had shrunk, as houses tend to do when one actually revisits one's childhood environs. But with Rushdie, some childhood experience perhaps made the house grow more mysterious and monstrous with years. May be he never revisited his childhood home. But autobiographical elements in Rushdie are hardly the point.

As for the magicians' ghetto in *Midnight's Children,* I was visiting Delhi, when Sanjay Gandhi's cleaning of the capital was in progress. Every night, government bulldozers would raze a whole row of hutments, and corrugated roofed shops that carried on a flourishing trade all along the major streets, and within a day or two shanties and corrugated-roofed shops would rise up on the same street or on a side street nearby. So Rushdie has merely indulged in metaphorical exaggeration of a very real situation.

Bariamma's dormitory is an analog for the joint family that was once typical of the sub-continent. Similarly, in *Shame,* Naveed's exponentially increasing numbers of children at each childbirth is only a metaphor for the subcontinent's population boom and it is not a pro-feminist's indictment of women's role in developing countries, as Linda thought.

I thought about the radical differences in our viewpoints, and came to another conclusion, not about graduate students such as Linda so much as about the current thrust towards literary theory. I am not denigrating the criticism that has been written about the feminization of the narrative or the feminization of Islam, for example, but all such focused readings diminish the text. For me, Rushdie's fiction is proof that we need to invert the old adage to say that in good literature, the sum of the parts in very much greater than the whole.

In the classroom, where our department has an accepted pedagogical practice that we incorporate literary theory into the course as early as the first year, I sometimes feel that we are taking away the spontaneity and reflexive pleasure of the students' reading experience by drawing them into the inner circle of theory and making them insiders who are conscious of all the literary jargon and critical baggage that usually comes with graduate school; by doing so we are in danger of making them outsiders to the sheer gut-centred pleasures of reading. So, the topic that interests me as an educator, is "at what stage of a student's programme is it most effective to introduce critical theory?" Clearly much depends on the reading repertoire of the average student but even at the graduate level, I have my reservations about the way our readings get into the Procrustean-bed, as I call it, of literary theory, where we stretch and pull the text to fit our literary position. I think Rushdie's texts have had more than their fair share of Procrustean critical tomes.

For me, open metaphors are the way to go. Never a full circle but a spiral that takes you a certain distance and then stops, leaving you to parachute yourself down as best you can. Rushdie's obsessive use of houses is an example of the potentials and pitfalls of sustaining a metaphor. It is indubitably there in every novel: Grimushome, Methwold Estate, Nishapur, Zogoiby's house, all are sprawling mansions with endless spaces in which the protagonist gets lost. The ghosts of the past seem to be the real masters while the living tenant is just a fugitive, held in thrall by the accumulated pressures of artifacts and collective memories. While I grant there might be a modicum of autobiography to his obsessive use of houses, I tend to think they recur as a continuing political metaphor. The reason why *The Moor's Last Sigh* fails for me is that the metaphor is too consistent and does not spiral upward but in a boring orbit.

But it is a great metaphor, for in the sub-continent "everything is family" as Clark Blaise says in his *Days and Nights in Calcutta.* In an interview published in *Kunapipi* in 1985, Rushdie says the same thing, I quote, "family is so central to life in India." and he goes on say, "What I wanted to say is that in this society . . . . There is a kind of Gogolian system where the ruling clan is minute, and politics is a kind of family quarrel."

Rushdie uses public politics and private relationships as a symbiotic and contrapuntal movement so that his novels embody the life of a community that Frederic Jameson says is the characteristic of third world literature. ("Third World Literature in the Era of Multinational Capitalism." *Social Text* 15,1986) Jameson goes on to say that third world novels tend to be national allegories.

Rushdie himself has been rather impatient when anyone mentions the allegorical content of his fiction. In that same interview in *Kunapipi,* he said that Indians tend to take everything as allegory, and he dismisses that preoccupation as unworthy of comment. But, despite Rushdie's impatience with the charge of allegory, it is all too clear that his writings are developed around an allegory.

Rushdie's allegorization succeeds most of the time because of the open-endedness of his allegories. He uses historical, real life events but never lingers long on any specific allegorical parallels, and develops open-ended metaphors instead. The Perforated Sheet, which is a significant image placed at the beginning of *Midnight's Children,* is a metaphor that works at many levels. At one level, it says that truth is always given to us piecemeal; at another level it says that a perforated sheet sustains the magic of life, for if everything is bared, there is only ennui instead of desire. Also, the perforated sheet is the metaphor for a narrative ploy which has used newspaper items to give the illusion of a vast canvas. Like the kaleidoscope and peep show images in *Midnight's Children,* references picked off newspapers, such as included in the long list of strange feats and tragedies that came upon the circle of the children of the special midnight that Saleem brought under his wing, reflect an expanse of historical repertoire of a vast and ancient country, whose collective life is what Saleem wishes to record. This is a structure that Rushdie has used in all his novels, and I confess, as I said, that it palled on me by the time I came to *The Moor's Last Sigh.* More of that later, if I have time.

Rushdie criticism, I said, is like dancing through a mine field. Almost everything in Rushdie can be read from two diametrically opposite directions. I open my talks on Indian themes (one of the exciting and boring things about Canadian multiculturalism is that one is often asked to be a spokesperson for one's ethno-culture) by saying that anything one says about India is both true and false. The same can be said of both Rushdie's portrayal of the sub-continent and of his thematic thrusts. In this context I have two issues that are in my tray of on-going research: Rushdie's feminism and Rushdie as brown sahib.

I have held that Rushdie's delineation of women is very sympathetic, and that he makes his women stronger than their men because he knows the strength of women. But one could argue with equal fervour that Rushdie is misogynistic.

I would like to read a paragraph from another of my papers where too I use the Rushdiesque style. As an aside, Once when I gave my creative writing class an assignment to write a poem in any one of the regular stanzaic forms, a student reeled off half a dozen perfect Spenserian stanzas, nine lines, Alexandrine and all, because she was taking a Spenser course at the time and the Spenserian beat was coming out of her ears, as she said. When I get into the Rushdie mode, this is what happens, as you can see when you hear the opening lines of my essay entitled "Impressive Women but the Chains are Real." *(the essay is included earlier in the volume.)*

I vacillated about the sequence in which I wanted to present my last two points, and I decided I would end on a pro-Rushdie note. So let me give you the other point first. I have changed, or rather am gradually changing my view of Rushdie. Like the persona I cited from my Giessen paper earlier, I too am wondering if Rushdie is with us-of-the-subcontinent or with them-imperialists. Is he a brown sahib? Was he ever a native son? In my first book, I name three categories of Indo-English writers – nineteenth and early twentieth century writers who aped the British style of writing, the native geniuses, like R.K. Narayan and Raja Rao, and native-aliens such as Kamala Markandaya.

I would place Salman Rushdie with the native aliens. My definition of native aliens is "writers born in India but whose education and life-style were so westernized that English is their first language and they are more conversant with Milton, Shakespeare and the Bible than with the Indian classics or Indian religious texts, and with the western way of life than with the everyday realities of life in India." When such a person leaves India, a certain shift in ethos occurs that accelerates the alienation of sensibility. Lest you think I am being adversarial, let me say that I too am a native alien, according to my definition. What I call our bi-cultural sensibility might well be called something less complimentary by others.

However, after reading Rushdie's Introduction and choice of material for the volume titled *Mirrorwork: 50 Years of Indian Writing,* (1997), I am getting convinced that Rushdie is now a brown sahib, and perhaps was always one.

For a conference next summer, I have sent in an abstract that is titled, "Not Post-Colonial Victim but Predatory Colonist: Flapping Eagle's True Colours in Rushdie's *Grimus.*"

My thesis is that Rushdie's *Grimus* and *The Moor's Last Sigh* are usually taken to be post-colonial protests against power structures, and majority domination of minorities etc., with Flapping Eagle and Moraes Zogoiby as the victims. But I would like to come to the novels from a diametrically opposite side – that both Flapping Eagle and the Moor can be seen as colonists in search of empires, who destroy cultures with their egocentric and primitive aggressiveness. This might not have been Rushdie's intention, but a good author often records more than he intends, and Rushdie is a good author.

Finally, I have a thesis that I call Rushdie's reluctant romanticism. It is often said that Romanticism is the philosophy of idealistic youth and cynicism the voice of failed idealism; as Dylan Thomas says, "because their words had forked no lightning, they do not go gentle into the good night." I would say that in Rushdie's case, Romanticism is the last straw to which he reaches out to sustain him in his Gethsemane.

When we are young, violence and evil seem powerful and therefore attractive. Rebellion as an expression of idealism is attractive; for the same reason pessimism, rather than optimism, is attractive. Childhood to youth to age is a journey, and I don't want to say youth is immature, age mature. Chronometric time has little to do with this epistemological journey; some of us stay at one stage, some of us move very slowly, and often we move two steps forward, one step back.

My thesis is that when life was going well for Rushdie, he tended to highlight violence and pessimism. I think that the *fatwah* and ensuing realities drew Rushdie out from one phase of understanding to another; I see *Haroun* as stating where he is at now. Though *The Moor's Last Sigh* was published after *Haroun,* it was much earlier in the making, and therefore I place *Haroun* after *The Moor* in Rushdie's evolution. *Haroun is* the outcome of an awareness that we need flotation devices in order cope with life; traditional religions provide anchors; but atheistic writers can offer fiction as a flotation device that could work for them and for others. Rushdie stated in February 1989 that he tried to fill with fiction the hole in his heart left by his atheism; that, I quote, "Unable to accept the absolute unarguables of religion, I have tried to fill up the hole with literature . . . . Literature is where I go to find the highest and lowest places in human society and the human spirit, where I hope to find not absolute truth but the truth of the tale, of the imagination and of the heart." *(Rushdie File p. 62.)*

*Haroun is* simple, almost simplistic, but so is the Sermon on the Mount, and all its equivalents in various faiths.

I see *Haroun* as Rushdie's attempt at closure, an assertion, an affirmation that with the power of the imagination, with the power of story-telling, good might win out; or rather, as in every other religion, we needs must believe that Good shall win over Evil, because that is the only way we can cope with life.